THE MAGIC OF SUMMER & WINTER WEAVING

SUSAN KESLER-SIMPSON

STACKPOLE BOOKS

Essex, Connecticut

STACKPOLE BOOKS

An imprint of The Globe Pequot Publishing Group, Inc.
64 South Main Street
Essex, CT 06426
www.globepequot.com

Copyright © 2026 by Susan Kesler-Simpson
Photography by Eckhaus Images

All rights reserved. No part of this book may be reproduced in any form or by any electronic or mechanical means, including information storage and retrieval systems, without written permission from the publisher, except by a reviewer who may quote passages in a review.

The contents of this book are for personal use only. Patterns herein may be reproduced in limited quantities for such use. Any large-scale commercial reproduction is prohibited without the written consent of the publisher.

We have made every effort to ensure the accuracy and completeness of these instructions. We cannot, however, be responsible for human error, typographical mistakes, or variations in individual work.

British Library Cataloguing in Publication Information available

Library of Congress Cataloging-in-Publication Data available

ISBN 978-0-8117-7650-9 (paper : alk. paper)
ISBN 978-0-8117-7651-6 (electronic)

Printed in India

CONTENTS

Introduction 1

CHAPTER 1: The Most Important Chapter 2

CHAPTER 2: Reading the Treadling Charts 4

CHAPTER 3: Reversing Images 8

CHAPTER 4: Profile Drafts 10

CHAPTER 5: Multi-Pedal Treadling for Jack Looms 12

CHAPTER 6: Putting Different Images onto One Project 15

CHAPTER 7: The Problem of Too Many Shafts Rising 18

PROJECTS

Cat Wagging Tail 23	Snowflakes 105
Cat Sitting Pretty 25	Monsters and Robots 107
Kitty Butt 29	Christmas Ornaments 111
Fluffy-Tailed Bunnies 31	Christmas Trees 113
Flavors of Summer 35	Birdhouses 117
Lickety-Split 37	Christmas Wreath 119
It's Spicy 41	Candle and Holder 123
Play Me a Tune 43	Shamrocks 125
Jack-O'-Lantern 47	Scottish Thistle 129
Autumn Leaves 49	Owls 131
Pumpkin Patch 53	Sheep 135
Three Crosses 55	Butterflies 137
Scary Skulls 59	Snowmen 141
Dog Tales 61	Cupcakes 143
There's No Place Like Gnome 65	Dapper Dachshund 147
Santa Claus 67	Cows 149
Southwest Sunset 71	Honeybees 153
Desert Landscape 73	Vegetable Garden 155
Just a Green Garden Snake 77	Happy Hour 159
Rattlesnake 79	Teddy Bears 163
Umbrellas for a Rainy Day 83	Mushrooms 165
Christmas Stockings 85	Pigs 169
Spiders!!! 89	Red or White? 171
Tulips 91	Alpacas and Llamas 175
Blue Flowers 95	Musical Notes Scarf
Poppies 99	(bonus project for 16-shaft loom) 177
Footballs 101	

Acknowledgments and Resources 180

CHAPTER 2
Reading the Treadling Charts

The treadling graphs for this book can seem complex and confusing, so I would like to walk you through how to read the graphs. First, remember that the graphs are written so you can read/weave them from the top down. I've color coded the boxes to help you use the correct color thread. Also, along the side I've written what part of the image you will be weaving. Look at the example in Figure 2.1 from Lickety-Split.

Along the right side you will see the cone, flavor 1, flavor 2, and the cherry indicated. This information tells you exactly what you are weaving. The X's within the treadling pattern are colored to indicate what color thread you will be using. In some treadling patterns, you will change the colors, but having the colored boxes is helpful. Make sure you use a tabby thread after each pattern thread even though it is not indicated on the graph. Unless specified, the tabby thread is the same color and size as the warp thread.

Let's talk again about the tabby thread. In the Santa Claus treadling graph (Figure 2.2), the tabby is indicated throughout the entire treadling pattern. While this might help, it does make a long treadling pattern. You will notice that there are two sections—the nose and the eyes—in which there are two pattern threads and one tabby. This is correct and is explained in more detail in the Christmas Tree treadling graph (Figure 2.3).

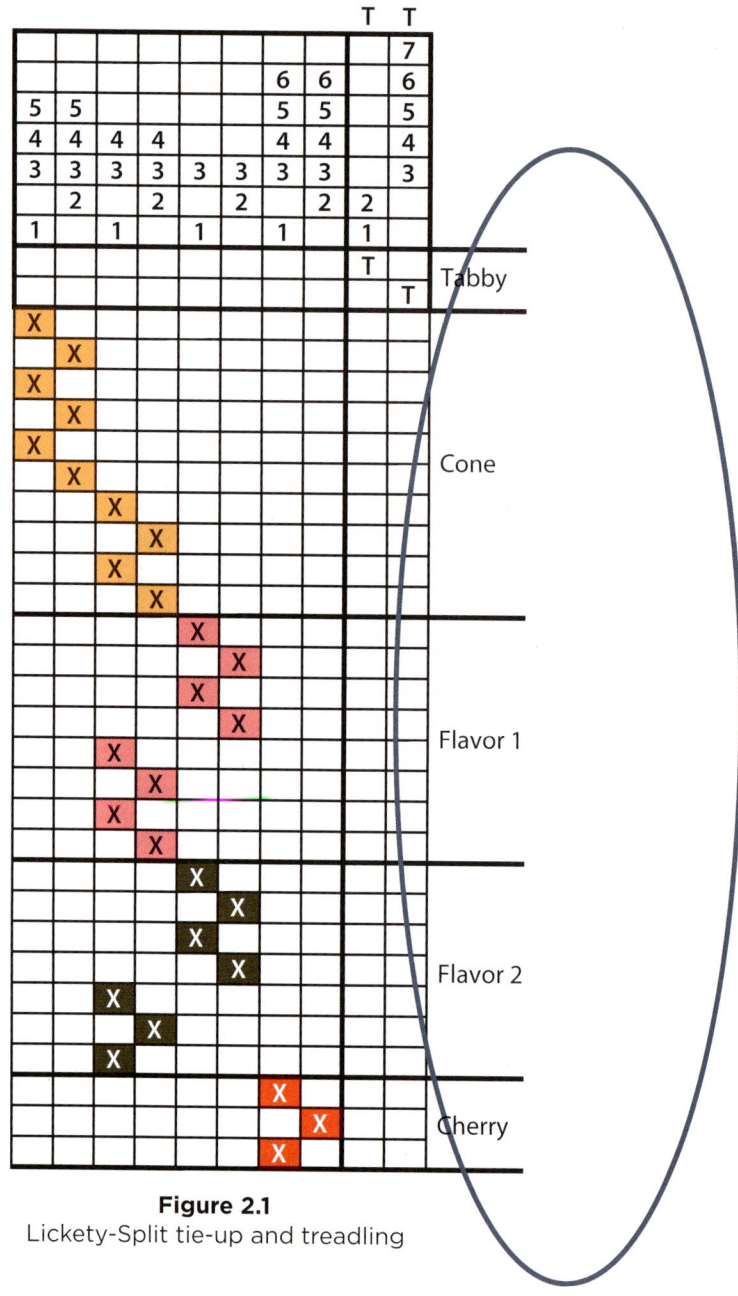

Figure 2.1
Lickety-Split tie-up and treadling

4 | READING THE TREADLING CHARTS

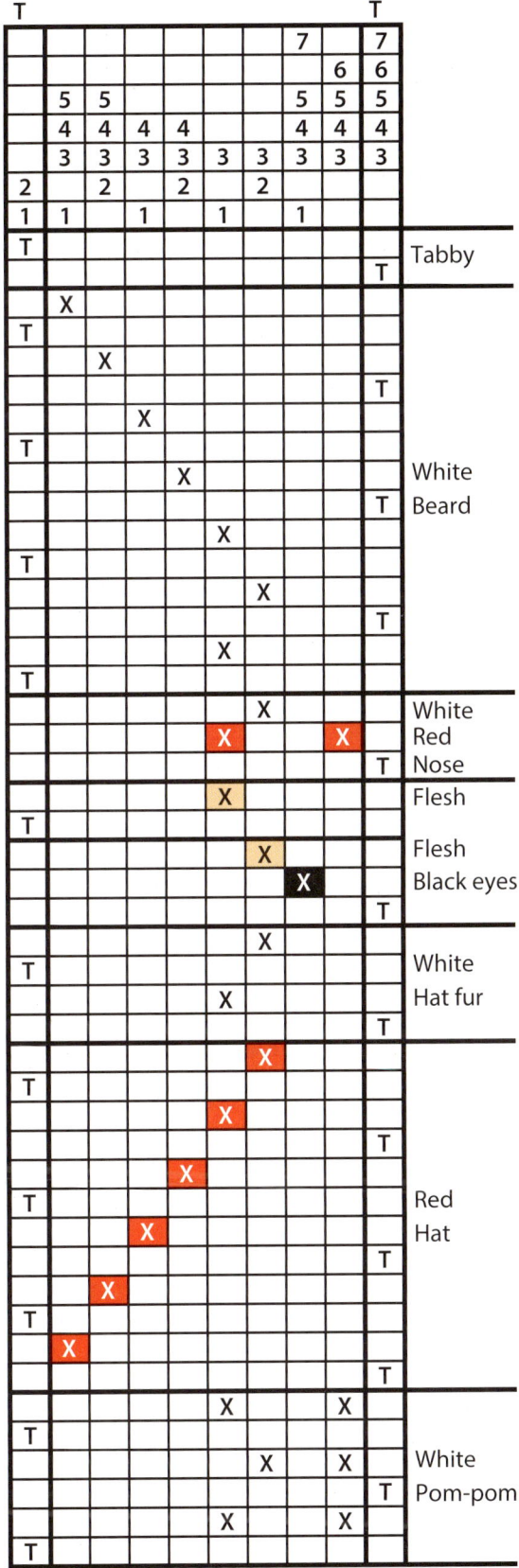

Figure 2.2
Santa Claus treadling

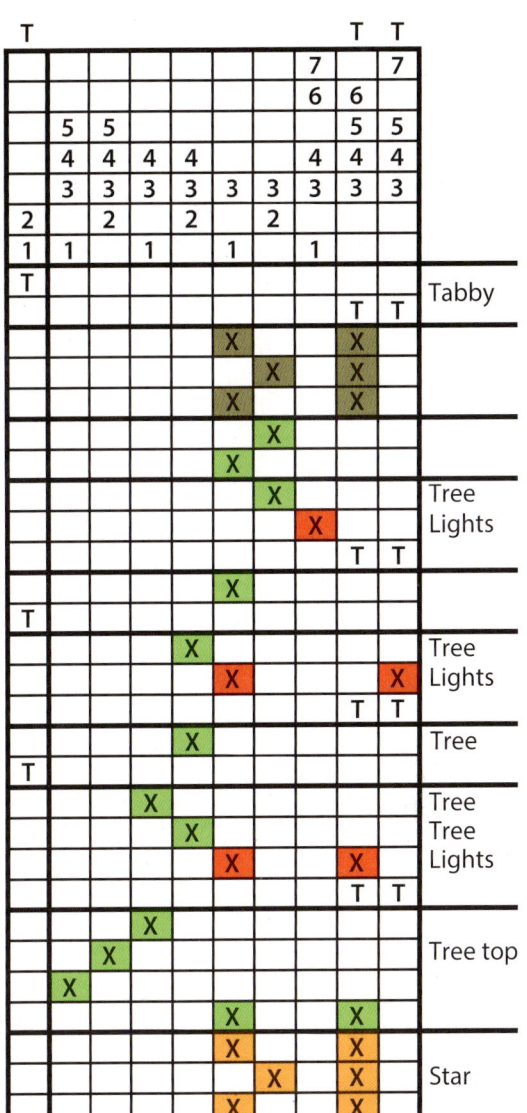

Figure 2.3
Christmas Tree treadling

Let's look at the treadling graph for the Christmas Tree. Here you will notice that I have not indicated the tabby at the beginning or throughout the chart *but only where more than one pattern thread is placed before the tabby is placed.* In the other areas of the graph, you will still be using a tabby after every pattern thread and you will still begin with the tabby treadle that raises shafts 1 and 2 after the first pattern thread. Not indicating the pattern thread throughout the graph is a space-saving practice.

Again, remember that in the treadling graphs you will always begin with the tabby that raises shafts 1 and 2 after the first pattern thread and then alternate tabbies. While the tabby threads may not be indicated throughout the graphs, you will still use a tabby after each pattern thread. In the

READING THE TREADLING CHARTS | 5

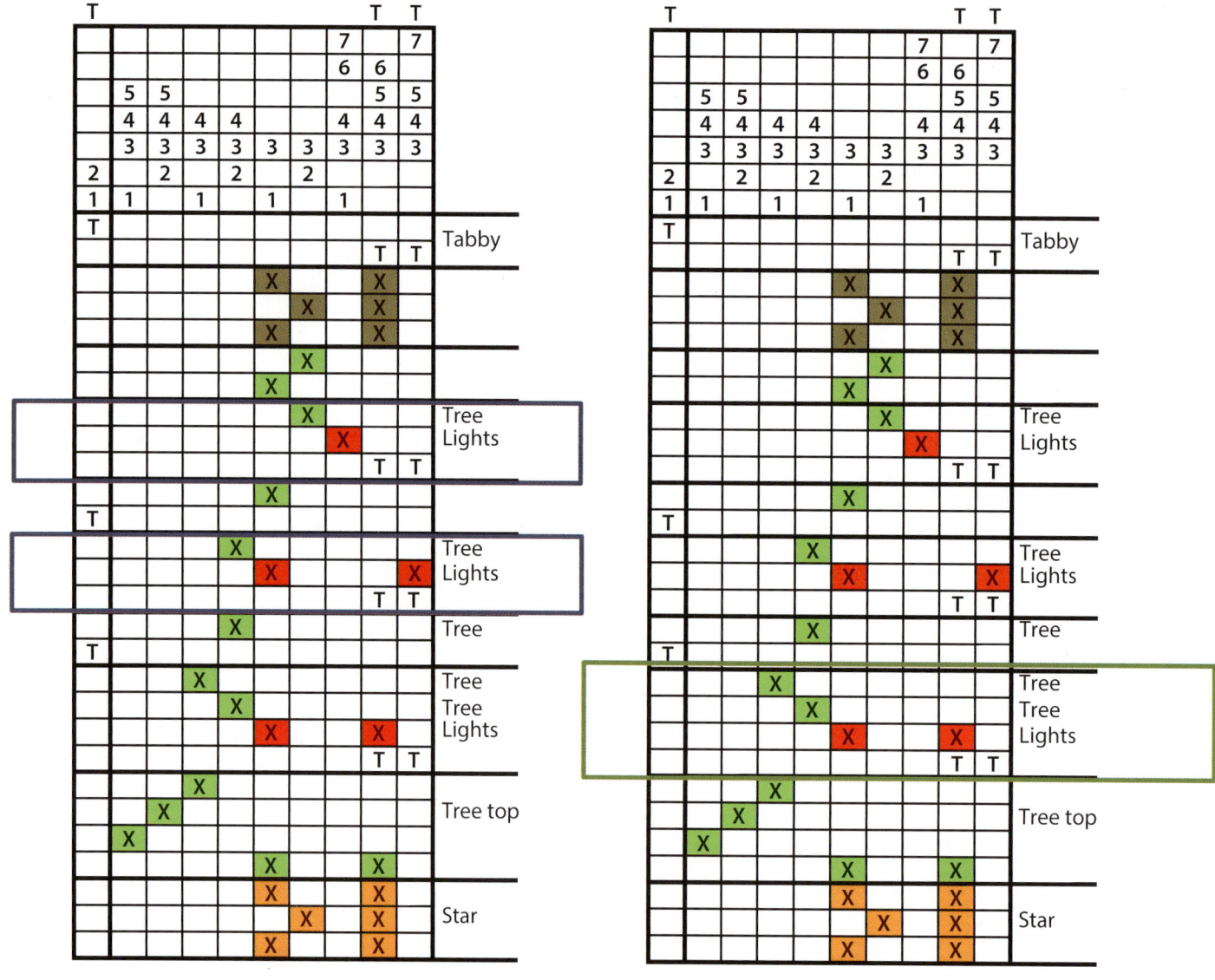

Figure 2.4
Christmas Tree treadling with two pattern threads and one tabby

Figure 2.5
Christmas Tree treadling with three pattern threads and one tabby area outlined

sections where there are insets in the motifs, I have given instructions as to which tabby is to be used. If you began the image correctly, you will automatically be ready to use the tabby that is indicated on the graph. If not, there is a mistake somewhere. Since it is very important that the tabby shown on the graph is the one that is used for the insets, be sure to correct your error before continuing.

Let's look at the Christmas Tree treadling graph (Figure 2.4). When weaving the insets, which are the red ornaments, you will be weaving two pattern threads and then one tabby. In Figure 2.4, these sections are outlined in blue.

In these two sections, you will weave the green thread, followed by the red thread, and then you will weave the tabby. Yes, you are putting two threads in before the tabby, but this is what allows the green of the tree to close around the red ornament.

There will also be times when you will need to weave three pattern threads before you put in a tabby. This also occurs in the Christmas Tree towel. Look at the section outlined in green in Figure 2.5. Two green pattern threads are woven, followed by one red pattern thread. *Then the tabby is woven*, which compacts the red under the last green pattern thread for the Christmas lights. In this example, it was very important to be using the correct tabby to get the proper look.

Remember: You will be using a tabby throughout the pattern even though it is not indicated on the graph.

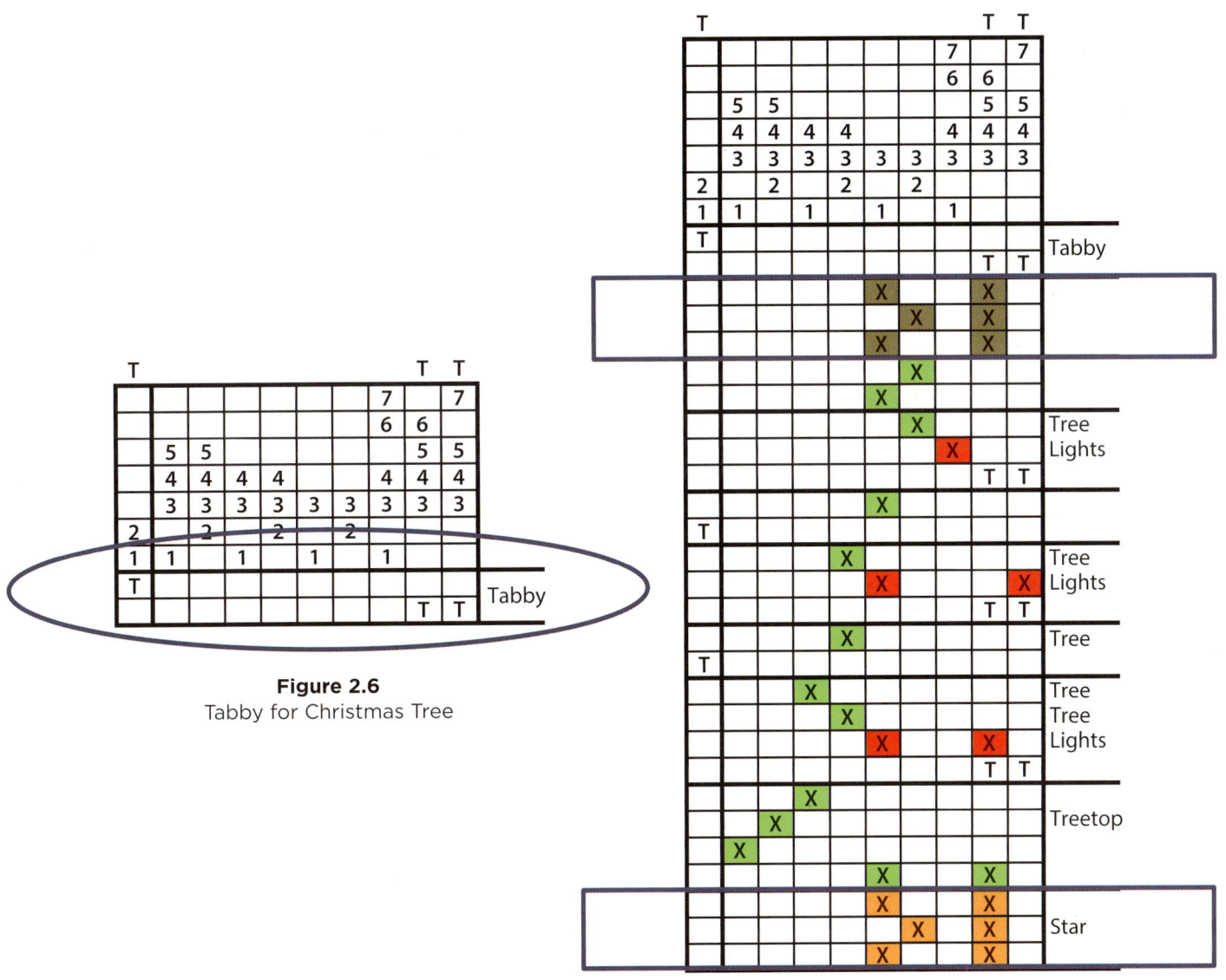

Figure 2.6
Tabby for Christmas Tree

Figure 2.7
Christmas Tree multi-pedal treadling

Remember: When I refer to a pattern thread, I'm using the 8/2 cotton, which requires two passes to make one pattern thread!

Remember: In my patterns I always refer to the tabby as being woven **after** the pattern thread.

Multi-Pedal Treadling

The next thing I want to point out is that there are times when, yes, you will be depressing two treadles to get either the first half or the second half of the tabby. Look at the tabby graph for the Christmas Tree (Figure 2.6).

The tabby on the left side of the graph uses one treadle to raise shafts 1 and 2. In order to get the tabby on the right, you will need to depress treadles 9 and 10. The combination of these two treadles raises shafts 3–7, which is your second tabby.

There will also be other times that you will use two treadles to get the proper combination of shafts to raise. Look again at the Christmas Tree graph (Figure 2.7).

In the two sections outlined in blue, you can see that you need to depress two treadles to get the correct combination of shafts to raise.

When weaving any project in this book, take your time thoroughly reading the treadling graph so that you understand it before you start.

READING THE TREADLING CHARTS | 7

CHAPTER 3
Reversing Images

Reversing the direction of the images is also affected by which tabby is used. The only towels in this book in which I reversed the images were the snake towels. It was necessary to do those for practical reasons. For the rest of the towels, the images are all facing one direction. There was a purpose behind this choice. First, it is easier to photograph the towels. Second, I knew that reversing images and the importance of the tabby needed to be addressed separately.

So, the question is: How do I reverse the image? My graphs are set up to read from top to bottom. I always have my tabby shuttle following my pattern shuttle, moving in the same direction; that is a preference. As discussed in the previous section, I always begin with the 1-2 tabby after the first pattern thread!

But let's say that now, instead of having multiple images on my towels, I want only one image at each end facing in opposite directions, or maybe I want to alternate the directions as I weave. Let's look at a very brief treadling graph with the tabby included (Figure 3.1). The tabby treadling begins with the pattern thread followed by the 1-2 tabby and alternates through the entire treadling sequence. In this example, I have outlined the last pattern thread and the tabby that *preceded it*! Why that tabby? Reversing the image would be reading the graph from the bottom up. So if you look at the X, which is the pattern thread, the tabby that would follow it would be the 1-2 tabby. Wonderful! Your image would be woven correctly.

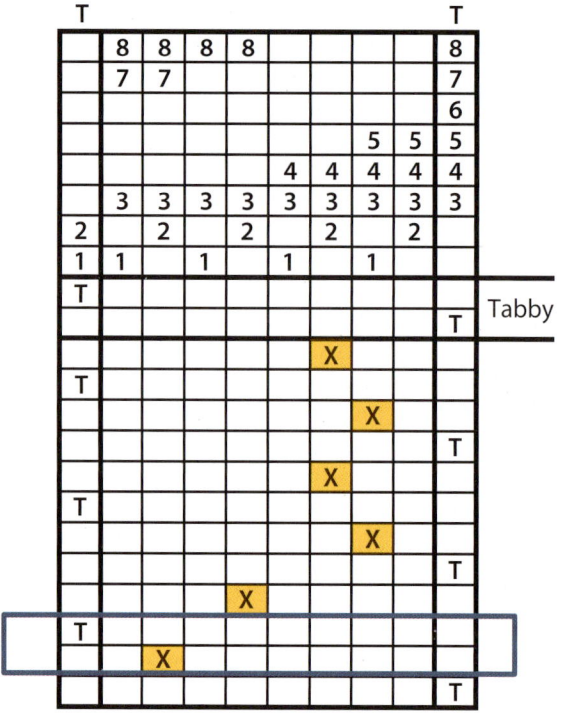

Figure 3.1
Last pattern thread with tabby

Now let's look at the next graph, where I've added one more pattern thread (Figure 3.2). Once again, the tabby treadling begins with the 1-2 tabby and alternates through the entire treadling sequence. I have outlined the last pattern thread and the tabby *that precedes it*! Remember that you are reversing the pattern, reading

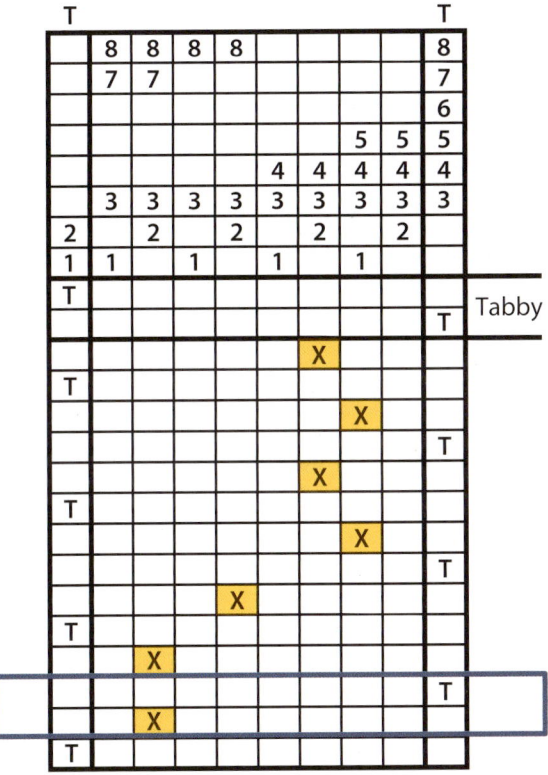

Figure 3.2
Added pattern thread

the graph from the bottom up. Now the first tabby would be the 3-4-5-6-7-8. In this case, I would start both threads from the right, once again keeping the shuttles always moving from the same direction. This time you will need to begin with the 3-4-5-6-7-8 tabby as your first tabby thread for your image to be correct.

Does it really make a difference? For some of the images, you would probably be ok, but for the more complex images—such as those with eyes, where the threads need to close around the eye properly—yes, it does make a difference. If you refer back to Chapter 1 and the images of the Santa Claus towels, you can see how using the incorrect tabby will affect your image.

I know it seems confusing, but it can be really simple. You do not need to write out all of the tabby threads as I did here to make it work. If you know you are planning to reverse your image, when you get to the *last pattern thread*, make a note of the tabby that was used before it. When you are ready to weave the reversed image, refer to that note, and now you know which tabby to start with. This will allow your reversed image to be correct.

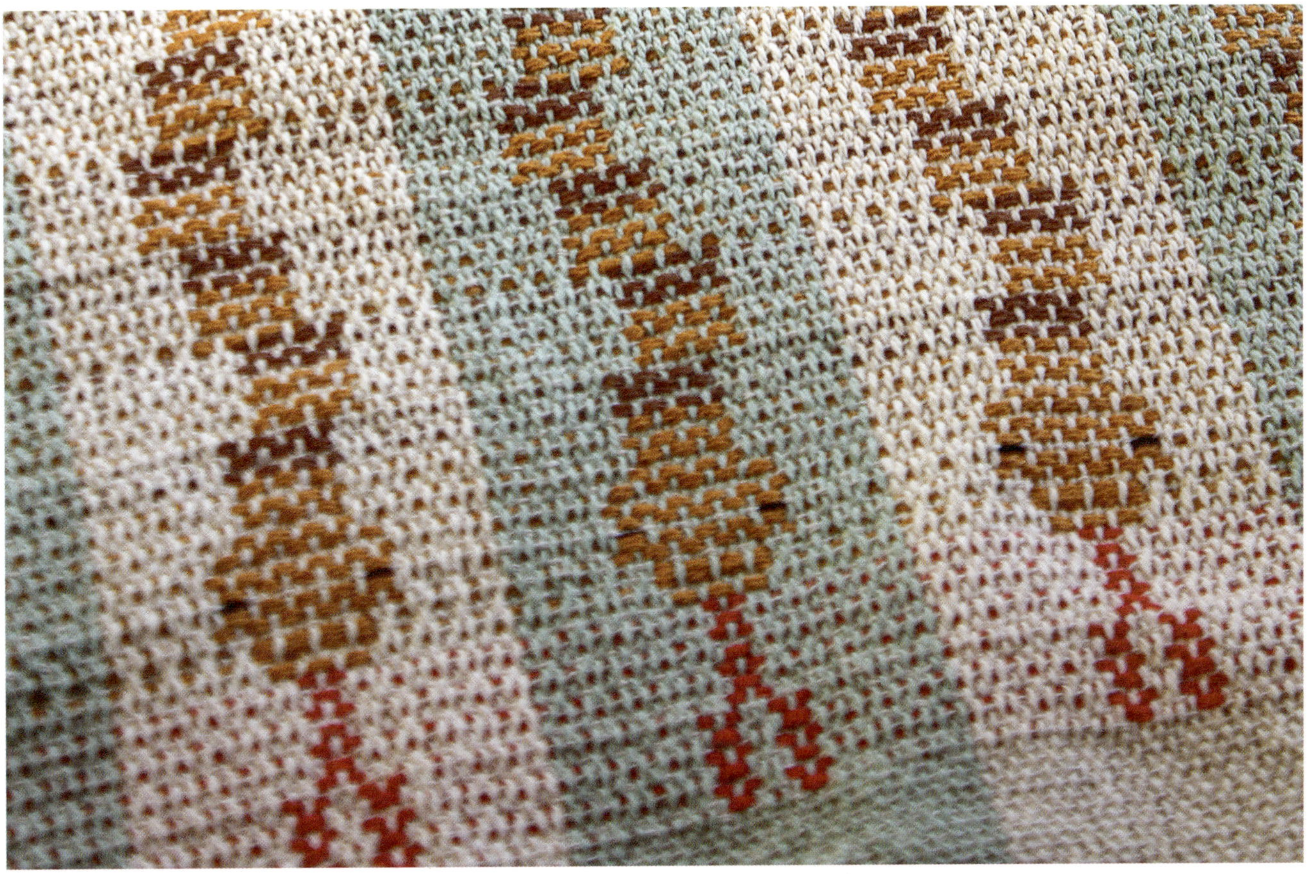

CHAPTER 4
Profile Drafts

Profile drafts can seem confusing, but once you understand what they are and why they are used, they are really quite easy. All of the projects in this book are based on summer and winter and use profile drafts. Let's begin!

Profile Threading

The easiest definition for profile drafts is that they are a form of shorthand for weavers. Instead of writing out a threading draft in full, they use blocks, which are lettered or darkened to indicate a *group* of threads. Below are the two threading blocks used for 4-shaft summer and winter. We will refer to them as Block A and Block B.

Profile drafts are most often written in the two ways shown in Figure 4.2. These profile drafts mean exactly the same thing: 3 Block As and 3 Block Bs.

In a profile draft, the blocks in Figure 4.1 are substituted into the profile draft. Where there was an A, the threading in Block A is substituted. Where there was a B, the threading in Block B is substituted. Figure 4.3 shows how these summer and winter blocks are substituted for the blocks in the profile draft. This graph shows the threading written out in full. You can see that the shorthand of profile drafts is a huge space saver.

Now let's look at 8 shafts. Figure 4.4 shows the 8-shaft profile written in the two different ways.

Figure 4.5 shows the threading pattern blocks for 8-shaft summer and winter. Once again, where there is an A block, the 4-thread A block is substituted. Where there is a B block, the 4-thread B block is substituted, and so forth. Figure 4.6 shows these substitutions.

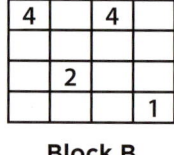

Figure 4.1
Block A and Block B for 4-shaft summer and winter

 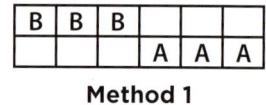

Figure 4.2
3 Block As and 3 Block Bs

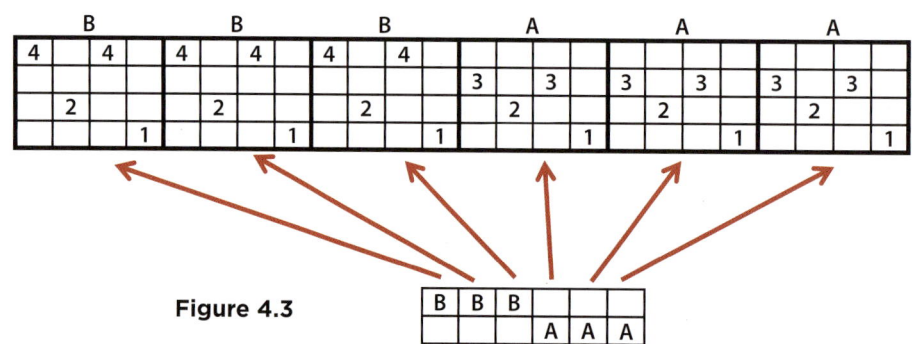

Figure 4.3

10 | PROFILE DRAFTS

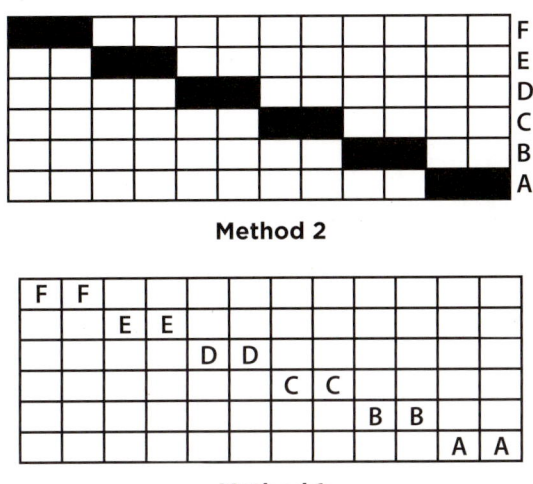

The first thing you should notice is that the full threading draft had to be put on two separate lines because it is so long. Working with large threading drafts can become very cumbersome, which is why profile drafts are so convenient. However, if you are threading your loom and find the profile draft confusing, use graph paper to fully write out the draft. I will often do this when using a profile draft—nothing to be embarrassed about! Make it easy for yourself!

I used profile drafts for the projects in this book. There are instances when the block is written out in full to indicate a color sequence of threads. The rules apply no matter how many shafts you are using.

Figure 4.4
Profile drafts for 8-shaft loom

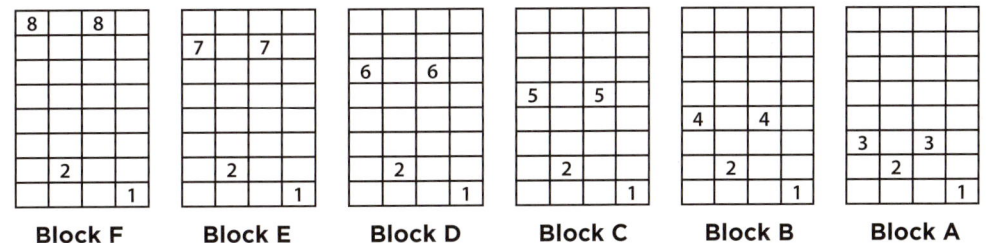

Figure 4.5
Blocks A–F for 8 shafts

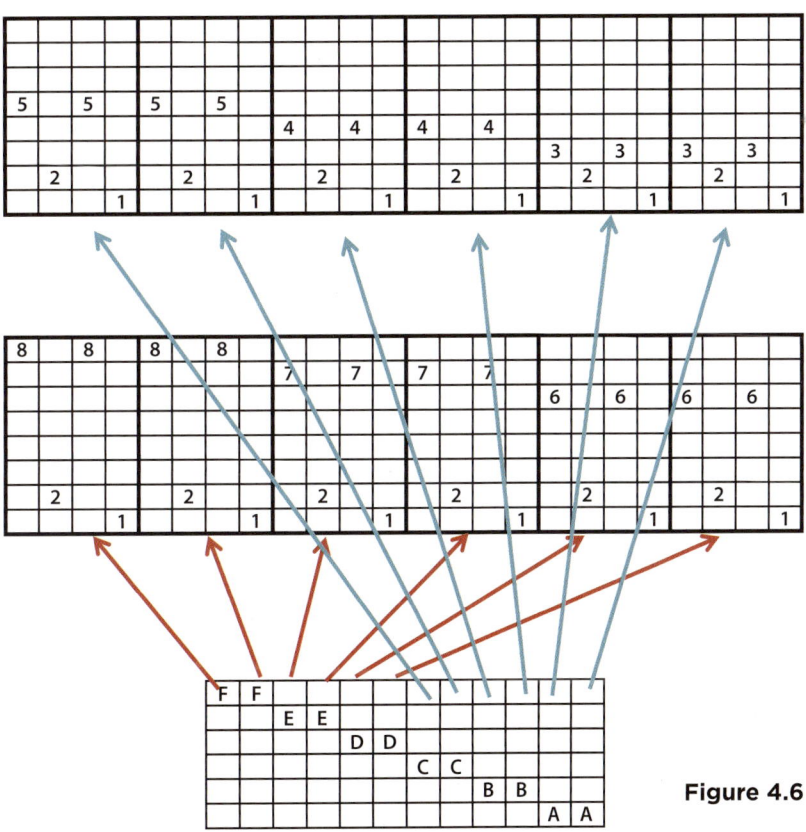

Figure 4.6

PROFILE DRAFTS | 11

CHAPTER 5

Multi-Pedal Treadling for Jack Looms

Let's talk about multi-pedal treadling and why it is necessary. We often think that the only time we would depress two treadles at the same time is when we have a direct tie-up loom. But that is not always the case. Let's look at the examples in Figure 5.1.

The original tie-up uses 12 treadles. An 8-shaft loom has only 10 treadles, so this tie-up simply won't work. Using Tim's Treadle Reducer, we are able to create a tie-up that is usable, but only by using *multi-pedal treadling*.

I'm going to break this idea down to help you understand. To make it easy to follow, I've isolated one set of the tie-up. In order to create the summer and winter motif/pattern, we will need to raise shafts 1-4-5-6 together and then 2-4-5-6 together. These are highlighted in Figure 5.2, which is in the original tie-up. Remember this point as we go forward.

Now we will break down the multi-pedal treadling in detail.

T	T										
	7					7	7	7	7	7	7
	6			6	6	6	6	6	6		
	5	5	5	5	5		5				
	4	4	4	4	4	5				4	4
	3	3	3					3	3	3	3
2			2		2		2		2		2
1		1		1		1		1		1	

T	T								
	7						7	7	7
	6			6			6	6	6
	5	5	5	5					
	4	4	4		4	4			
	3	3	3						3
2			2			2		2	
1		1			1		1		

Figure 5.1

T	T										
	7					7	7	7	7	7	7
	6			6	6	6	6	6	6		
	5	5	5	5	5	5	5				
	4	4	4	4	4					4	4
	3	3	3					3	3	3	3
2			2		2		2		2		2
1		1		1		1		1		1	

Figure 5.2

T	T									
	7						7	7	7	
	6			6			6	6		
	5	5	5	5						
	4	4	4		4	4				
	3	3	3						3	
2			2			2		2		
1		1			1		1			
X										Tabby
	X									
		X								
			X							
			X							
		X								
				X	X					←
				X		X				
				X		X				
				X	X					
				X			X			
				X				X		
				X				X		
				X			X			

Figure 5.3

Figure 5.3 shows the *skeleton tie-up* with just a partial treadling sequence. The treadling has been highlighted with a red arrow and pink blocks. If you follow the first line of X's to the tie-up, you will see that when you depress the first highlighted treadle, you are raising shafts 5 and 6. The second treadle raises 1 and 4. By depressing these treadles together, you are raising 1, 4, 5, and 6. Look back at the original tie-up with highlights, and you will see that you have accomplished just what is needed.

Now we will move to the second part of the pattern. In Figure 5.4, when you depress the first highlighted treadle, you are raising shafts 5 and 6. When depressing the second treadle, you are raising shafts 2 and 4. By depressing them together, you are raising shafts 2, 4, 5, and 6. Looking at the original tie-up with highlights, you can see that you have accomplished the second half of the pattern. One of the rules for the summer and winter X's or O's treadling pattern is that each set of pattern shafts must include shaft 1 followed by the same set including shaft 2. By doing multi-pedal treadling, this has been accomplished.

One more example! Look at Figure 5.5: the original tie-up graph with a different set of shafts chosen. In this section, you will need to raise shafts 1-5-6-7 and then shafts 2-5-6-7. This is accomplished in Figure 5.6. If you look at the line indicated by the red arrow and the pink column up to the tie-up, you can see that with one treadle you are raising shafts 5 and 6, and with the other treadle you are raising 1, 6, and 7. Shaft 6 is raised by both treadles. That is not a problem, so don't let it throw you. This situation is not unusual in skeleton tie-ups. The main thing is that the result of using these two treadles together is raising shafts 1-5-6-7, which is exactly what you needed.

Now we move on to create the second half of the pattern. In Figure 5.7, the red arrow lines up with the next pair of treadles. The same shafts are being raised, with the exception of shaft 2 instead of shaft 1. This completes the X's or O's summer and winter treadling.

Multi-pedal treadling is very common in summer and winter, especially as the motifs and tie-ups become more complex. Multi-pedal treadling is used quite a bit in this book. Just be sure to carefully read the treadling so you know where it is indicated.

T	T									
	7						7	7	7	
	6			6			6	6		
	5	5	5	5						
	4	4	4		4	4				
	3	3	3						3	
2			2			2		2		
1		1			1		1			
X										Tabby
	X									
		X								
			X							
			X							
		X								
				X	X					
				X		X				←
				X		X				
				X	X					
				X			X			
				X				X		
				X				X		
				X			X			

Figure 5.4

T	T										
	7					7	7	7	7	7	7
	6			6	6	6	6	6	6		
	5	5	5	5	5	5	5				
	4	4	4	4	4					4	4
	3	3	3					3	3	3	3
2			2		2		2		2		2
1		1		1		1		1		1	

Figure 5.5

T	T									
	7						7	7	7	
	6			6			6	6		
	5	5	5	5						
	4	4	4		4	4				
	3	3	3						3	
2			2			2		2		
1		1			1		1			
X										Tabby
	X									
		X								
			X							
			X							
		X								
				X	X					
				X		X				
				X		X				
				X	X					
				X			X			←
				X				X		
				X				X		
				X			X			

Figure 5.6

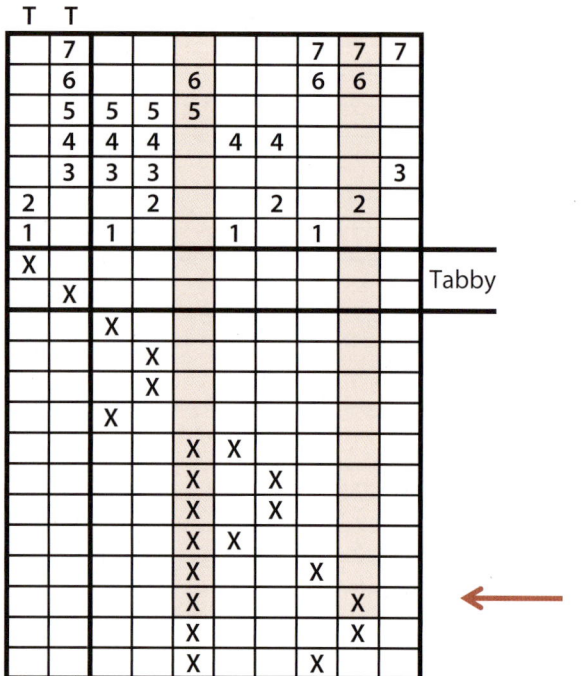

Figure 5.7

There is one more very important detail to remember about skeleton tie-ups and multi-pedal treadling: When you have used Tim's Treadle Reducer to create a new tie-up, remember that you will have to redesign the treadling sequence. This program will tell you what treadles need to be combined. I use Fiberworks Bronze in my designing, so I will create a new image with the original threading sequence and the skeleton tie-up. Then, following the instructions in Tim's Treadle Reducer, I will put in the new treadling sequence. This method allows me to make sure that I've followed the instructions correctly and have the same image/motif that was created with the original tie-up.

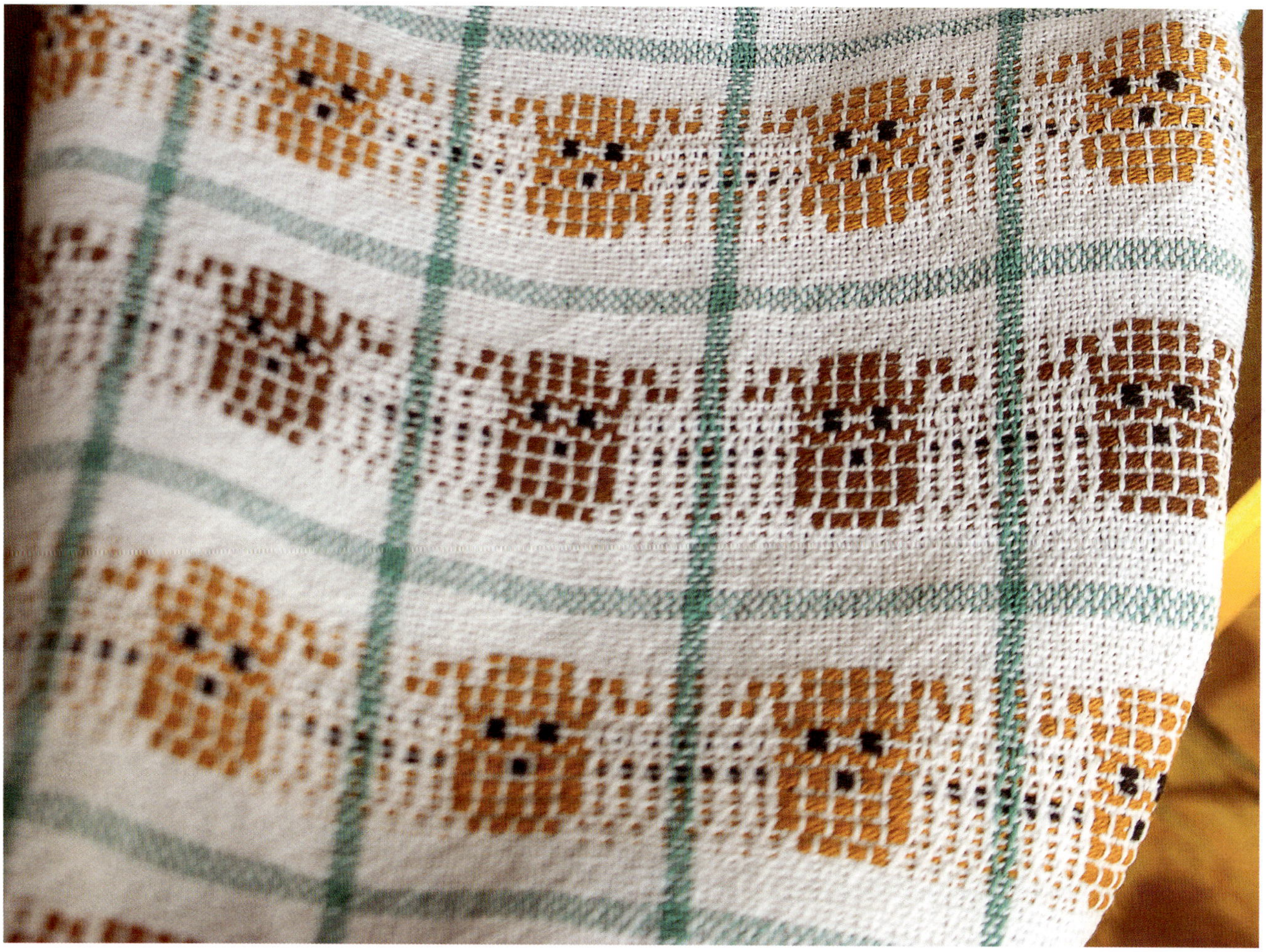

CHAPTER 6
Putting Different Images onto One Project

Now you have looked at the different projects in the book and chosen your favorites, but, instead of weaving separate towels, you want to combine images onto one towel or table runner. Can you do this? Of course! But how do you know which images can be combined?

	3		3
		2	
			1

Block A

Figure 6.1

The first thing to know is that Block A, which is shown in full in Figure 6.1, is the block that separates the images. It is not used to create flowers, Christmas trees, or any of the images (with the exception of the Spider Towels).

This leaves the rest of the blocks—B through F—as design blocks. All of the projects use a variety of Blocks B through F for the design. The vertical stripes also use Block A. You could easily eliminate the vertical stripes or make them wider, narrower, or fancier.

Our first example will be a project that used three flower images

Figure 6.2

PUTTING DIFFERENT IMAGES ONTO ONE PROJECT | 15

(Figure 6.2). Look at the threading graphs (Figures 6.3, 6.4, and 6.5) for the three different flowers with just the *design* blocks highlighted in yellow. Notice that in each of the graphs the design area is identical! This means that it is very simple to use all three flowers on one towel or runner. Only the treadling and the tie-up would change (as detailed later).

Could you add a butterfly to your garden of flowers? Let's look at the design area of the threading for the butterfly (Figure 6.6). In this threading, you can see that Block F is used in the butterfly image. Because of the addition of Block F, you would not be able to include the butterfly with your flowers.

We will look at one more combination of images (Figure 6.7). This set would get us ready for some wonderful Christmas towels to give as gifts.

Figures 6.8, 6.9, and 6.10 show three threading graphs with the design blocks highlighted in yellow. All of these threading graphs use Blocks B through E for the design area, so you can easily use these three images on one project. Just select your warp color carefully to make sure that your images will stand out.

You will also notice in Figure 6.7 that these images were reversed in the second half of the project. This arrangement would be great for a table runner or even a scarf. Just make sure you read Chapter 3 on how to reverse the images before you start.

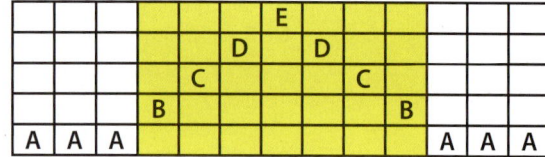

Figure 6.3
Tulips

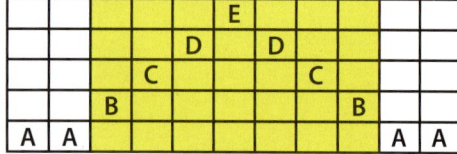

Figure 6.4
Blue Flowers

Figure 6.5
Poppies

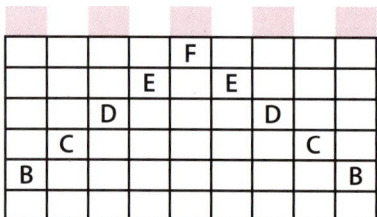

Figure 6.6
Butterfly

Figure 6.7

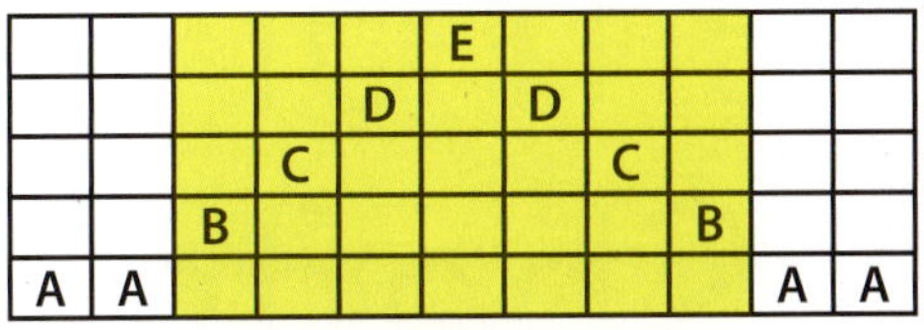

Figure 6.8
Christmas Ornament

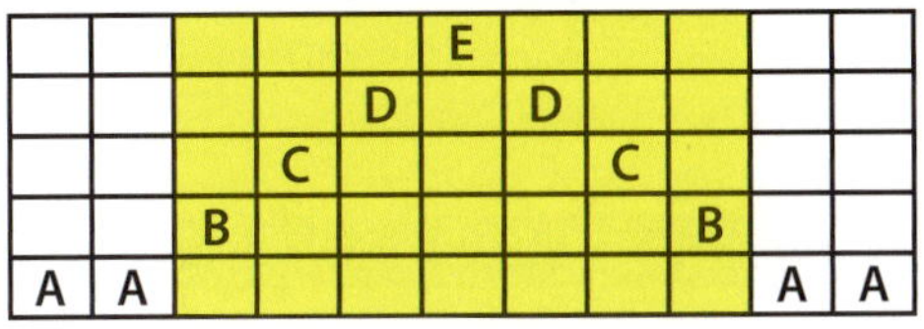

Figure 6.9
Christmas Tree

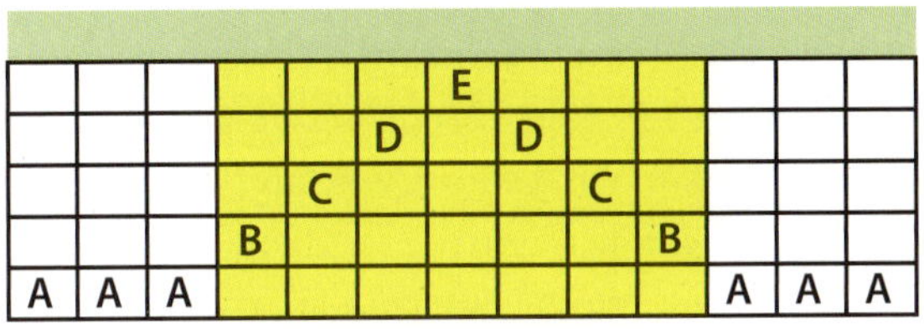

Figure 6.10
Santa Claus

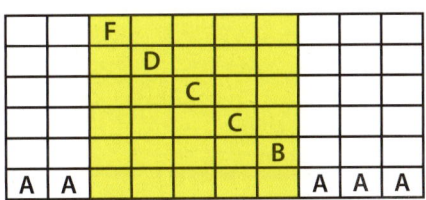

Figure 6.11
Christmas Stocking

Figure 6.12
Christmas Wreath

Unfortunately, you would not be able to use the Christmas Stocking or the Christmas Wreath (Figures 6.11 and 6.12), as these threading graphs are very different from the Santa Claus, Christmas Tree, and Christmas Ornament.

One more comment on this idea: While the threading graphs may be the same, the tie-up and treadling are different for each image. The different treadling does not pose a problem. But the tie-ups! Oh my! If you are planning to use a floor loom, you will have to change the tie-up each time you switch to a different image. For many of us, this is not easy. Using different images on one project is easiest with a table loom. Just read the graphs carefully to make sure you raise all of the necessary shafts.

PUTTING DIFFERENT IMAGES ONTO ONE PROJECT | 17

CHAPTER 7

The Problem of Too Many Shafts Rising

One of the problems I ran into while working on the projects for this book was that, at times, I would have extras shafts rising when I depressed a treadle. This didn't happen every time, but it sure was a nuisance when it did. I had to come up with a solution.

I have a 42-inch (106.7 cm) LeClerc Nilus loom and remembered that it has springs to which the treadles are attached, which help pull the shaft back down. The Baby Wolf does not have these, but I found at the back of the loom a series of holes each lining up with a treadle. Now I had a solution! I used ¼-inch (0.6 cm) elastic and cut pieces 12 inches (30.5 cm) long. Next, I made a large knot at one end, making sure it was large enough to not pull through the hole (Figure 7.1). Then the elastic piece was threaded through the hole and another large knot created at the opposite end (Figure 7.2). I now leave

Figure 7.1

Figure 7.2

these elastic pieces on the loom all the time.

Now you are ready to tie up your treadles. When the problem of too many shafts rising occurs, start attaching the elastic pieces to the treadles in the same manner that you would attach a shaft (Figure 7.3). Sometimes you need only a few and other times all of them. This method will eliminate the problem of too many shafts rising.

Figure 7.3

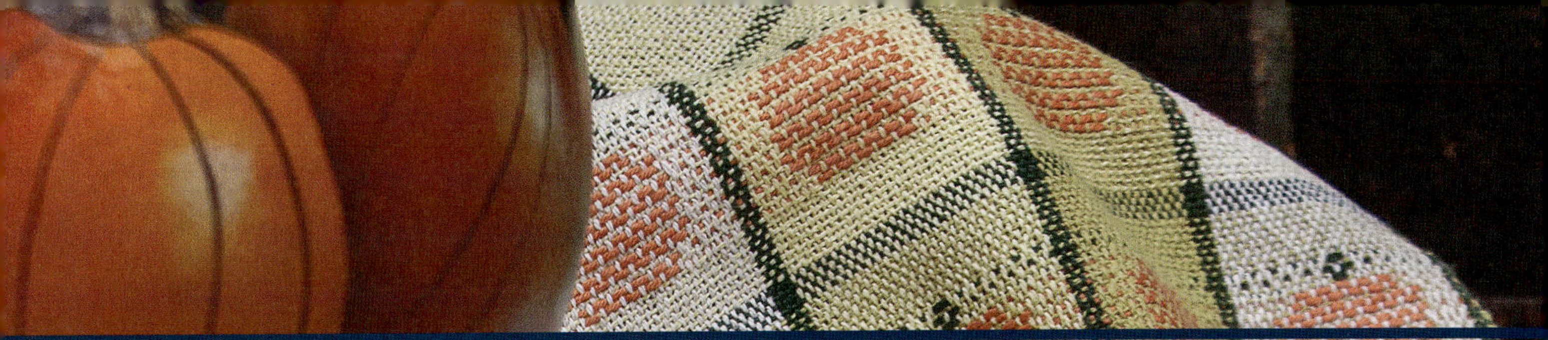

PROJECTS

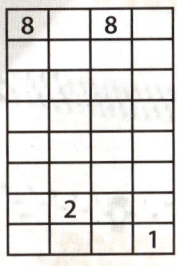 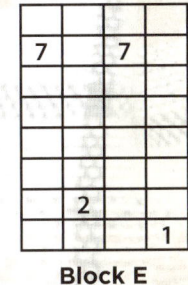 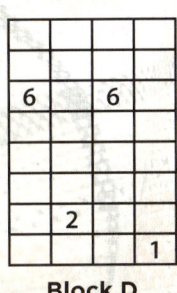 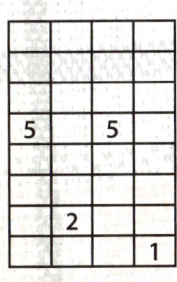 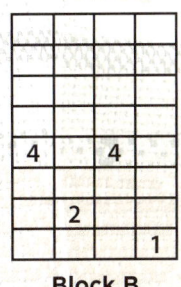 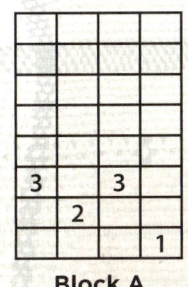

Block F   Block E   Block D   Block C   Block B   Block A

Block Key

Cat Wagging Tail

This is the first in a series of three cats, each with a different personality. This particular kitty is sitting at the window, watching the birds and squirrels. No doubt he's thinking about how he could catch them if *only* he could figure out how to get outside. While this project is set up as a set of towels, you could easily change threads, increase the size of the project, and make a beautiful table runner. This is a perfect gift for the cat lover in your home.

Begin your towels with 3 inches (7.6 cm) of Baby Blue plain weave. Then weave 4 passes of White plain weave, followed by 0.5 inches (1.3 cm) of Baby Blue plain weave. Next weave the first row of cats. When you have finished this row, weave 0.5 inches (1.3 cm) of Baby Blue plain weave, followed by 4 passes of White plain weave. Repeat this process until you have woven 5 rows of cats. Finish with 3 inches (7.6 cm) of Baby Blue plain weave. Weave 4 passes of a high-contrast color to separate the towels, and then weave the second towel. Finish your towels with a rolled hem.

Note: Be sure to read Chapter 1, "The Most Important Chapter," before beginning any project in this book.

Dimensions: 15 × 23 inches (38.1 × 58.4 cm)

Warp
Sett: 20 epi, 10 dent reed, 2 threads per dent
Length: 3-yard (2.7-m) warp
Threads: 8/2 Cotton Clouds Aurora Earth
- White: 50 ends (includes 2 floating selvedges), 175 yards (160 m)
- Baby Blue: 252 ends, 800 yards (731.5 m)

Weft
8/2 Cotton Clouds Aurora Earth
- Baby Blue: 500 yards (457.2 m)
- White: 35 yards (32 m)

Pattern thread (for cats): 8/2 Cotton Clouds Aurora Earth: Navy Blue, 300 yards (274.3 m)

Threading
Border: 1 time
Alternate Motifs A
    and B: 6 times
Motif A: 1 time
Border: 1 time

Motif B
4 ends

Motif A
36 ends

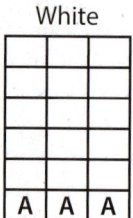

Border
12 ends

Treadling
1 full repeat is 1 cat.
Use tabby.

Tie-up and Treadling

Cat Sitting Pretty

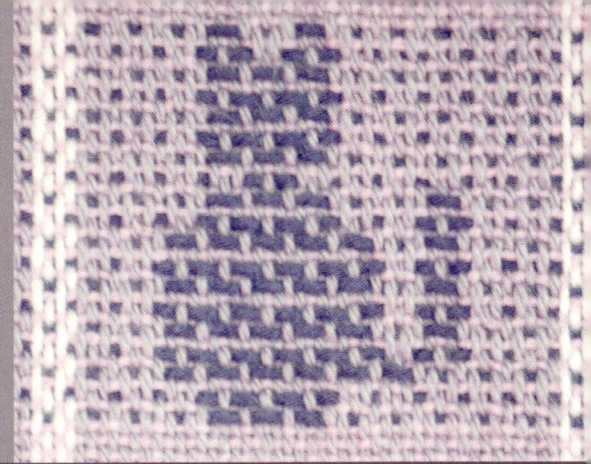

This is the second cat in the series. This sweetie is waiting, ever so patiently, for you to give him his lunch. Be quick, though—that sweet face won't last long! I filled these towels with cats, although you could weave just one row. You could also add or change borders. I began and ended each towel with 2.5 inches (6.4 cm) of Lavender plain weave. Then I wove the first row of cats. I wove 0.5 inches (1.3 cm) of Lavender plain weave between each row. In each towel, there are 10 rows of cats. Weave 4 passes of a high-contrast thread after the first towel, and then weave the second towel. Finish each towel with a rolled hem.

Note: Be sure to read Chapter 1, "The Most Important Chapter," before beginning any project in this book.

Dimensions: 17 × 25 inches (43.2 × 63.5 cm)

Warp
Sett: 20 epi, 10 dent reed, 2 threads per dent
Length: 3-yard (2.7-m) warp
Threads: 8/2 Cotton Clouds Aurora Earth
- Lavender: 308 ends, 950 yards (868.7 m)
- White: 34 ends (includes 2 floating selvedges), 120 yards (109.7 m)

Weft and Tabby
8/2 Cotton Clouds Aurora Earth
- Lavender: 600 yards (548.6 m)
- Purple: 400 yards (365.8 m)

Threading
Full Motif: 7 times
Partial Motif: 1 time

White

Partial Motif
4 ends

White

Full Motif
48 ends

Tie-up and Treadling

Treadling
Use tabby.

- Tabby
- Bottom of cat
- Body
- Neck
- Head
- Ears

CAT SITTING PRETTY | 27

Kitty Butt

This is the last in the cat series and oh, so fun to weave. Those of us who are owned by cats have seen this view so very often! I was raised on a dairy farm with many, many cats, and every morning there would be a cat convention outside the back door. Then Dad would head to the barn with all the cats following—so this is the image that remains in my head!

Begin your towel with 1.5 inches (3.8 cm) of White tabby. Next weave 3.5 inches (8.9 cm) of Nile Green tabby. Then weave 4 passes of Champagne tabby, followed by 0.5 inches (1.3 cm) of White tabby. Now you will weave your first row of cat butts with a White tabby. Follow with 0.5 inches (1.3 cm) of White tabby and then 4 passes of Champagne tabby.

At this point, I wove 3.25 inches (8.3 cm) of Nile Green tabby, although you could add more rows of cats if you like instead of this space. Repeat this process until you have completed all 3 rows of cats. Weave 0.5 inches (1.3 cm) of White tabby and 4 passes of Champagne tabby. Finally, weave 3.5 inches (8.9 cm) of Nile Green tabby. Weave 4 passes of a high-contrast color, and then weave the second towel. For my second towel, I used the Nile Green for the beginning and end. Finish your towels with a rolled hem.

Note: Be sure to read Chapter 1, "The Most Important Chapter," before beginning any project in this book.

Dimensions: 16 × 24 inches (40.6 × 61 cm)

Warp
Sett: 20 epi, 10 dent reed, 2 threads per dent
Length: 3-yard (2.7-m) warp
Threads: 8/2 Cotton Clouds Aurora Earth
- White: 144 ends, 440 yards (402.3 m)
- Nile Green: 144 ends, 440 yards (402.3 m)
- Champagne: 38 ends (includes 2 floating selvedges), 125 yards (114.3 m)

Weft and Tabby
8/2 Cotton Clouds Aurora Earth
- White: 275 yards (251.5 m)
- Nile Green: 275 yards (251.5 m)
- Champagne: 30 yards (27.4 m)

Pattern thread: 8/2 Cotton Clouds Aurora Earth: Dark Green, 200 yards (182.9 m)

Threading

Repeat Full Motif: 4 times
Partial Motif: 1 time

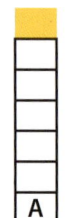

Partial Motif
4 ends

Full Motif
80 ends

White

Tie-up and Treadling

Treadling
Use tabby.

									T	T	
8	8									8	
								7		7	
				6	6					6	
						5	5			5	
4	4					4	4			4	
3	3	3	3	3	3	3	3			3	
	2		2		2				2		
1		1		1					1		
								T			Tabby
									T		
X			X								
	X			X							
X			X								Legs
	X			X							
X			X								
	X			X							
		X									
			X								
		X									
			X								
		X									Body
			X								
		X									
	X										
X											
	X					X					
X						X					
	X					X					
X						X					Tail
		X			X						
	X			X							
				X							
	X			X							

Fluffy-Tailed Bunnies

These towels would be fun for your Easter celebration. You could also change the colors and create a stunning baby blanket. How about making a couple of towels for burp cloths? That would be a wonderful gift set! I have given you the colors used for this set of towels; however, in the yardages you are given what is needed for just one row of bunnies. These towels can be a great stash buster. I began with the color Beauty Rose and repeated that color as the last bunny. The other colors are used only one time.

Begin by weaving 3.5 inches (8.9 cm) of plain weave in Yellow. Next, weave 0.5 inches (1.3 cm) of White, and then weave your first row of bunnies. It is very important that you follow the tabby sequence when weaving the bunnies. The tabby sequence is indicated in the treadling through the tail. After you have finished the tail section, continue to alternate the tabby thread throughout the rest of the bunny. After you have woven your bunnies, weave another 0.5 inches (1.3 cm) of plain weave. You will weave the next row of bunnies with the White tabby. Alternate the tabby color throughout the towel. You will weave a total of 5 rows of bunnies and end with 3.5 inches (8.9 cm) of plain weave in White.

The bunny tails were created with rayon chenille for a fuzzy look. You can also use 8/2 cotton in White or in color for something different.

Weave 4 passes of a high-contrast thread, and then weave your second towel. Finish your towels with a rolled hem.

Note: Be sure to read Chapter 1, "The Most Important Chapter," before beginning any project in this book.

Dimensions: 17 × 23 inches (43.2 × 58.4 cm)

Warp
Sett: 20 epi, 10 dent reed, 2 threads per dent
Length: 3-yard (2.7-m) warp
Threads: 8/2 Cotton Clouds Aurora Earth
- White: 154 ends (includes 2 floating selvedges), 475 yards (434.3 m)
- Yellow: 192 ends, 600 yards (548.6 m)

Weft
Tabby: 8/2 Cotton Clouds Aurora Earth
- White: 300 yards (274.3 m)
- Yellow: 300 yards (274.3 m)

Per row of bunnies: 8/2 Cotton Clouds Aurora Earth: 25 yards (22.9 m)
- Rayon Chenille (tail): 5 yards (4.6 m)
- Colors: Turk, Purple, Rose Red, Beauty Rose, Winter Green

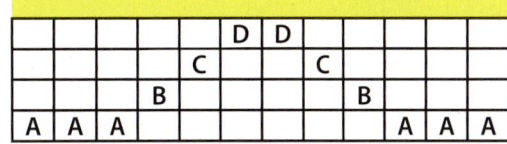

Motif B
48 ends

Motif A
48 ends

Border
4 ends

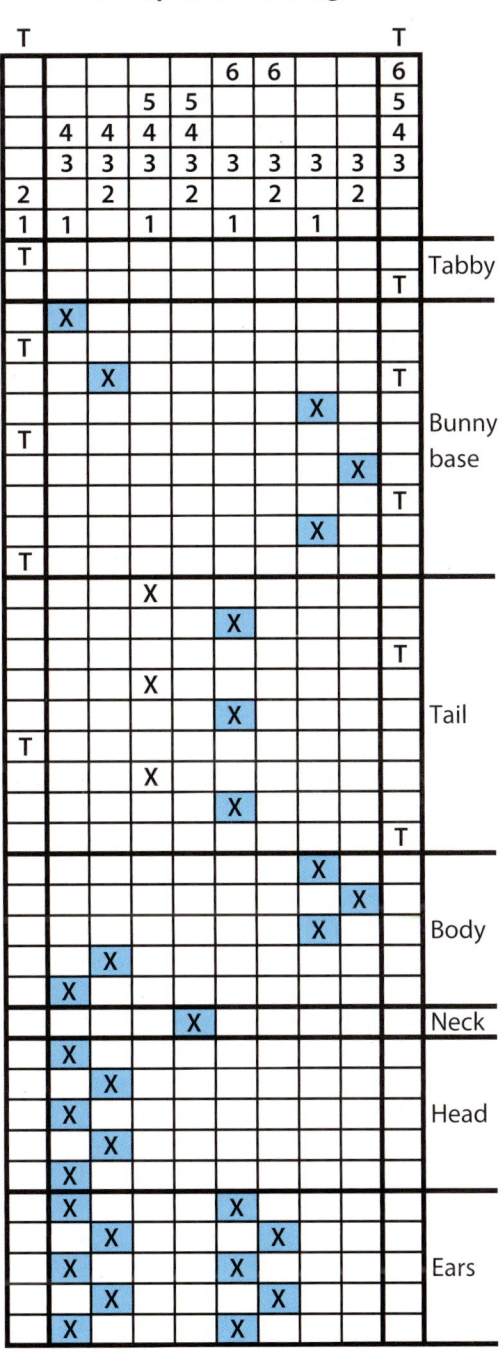

Tie-up and Treadling

Tabby
Bunny base
Tail
Body
Neck
Head
Ears

Threading
Border: 1 time
Alternate Motifs A and B: 3 times
Motif A: 1 time
Border: 1 time

Treadling
The tabby sequence is indicated **through** the tail. After completing the tail, continue alternating the tabby thread.

FLUFFY-TAILED BUNNIES | 33

Flavors of Summer

Hot, steamy summer days and frozen popsicles melting and running down the arm—these are the memories of childhood! Not to mention the wonderful flavors of cherry, orange, grape, and blueberry. My favorite was always cherry. These towels are perfect for wiping up those drips at your summer picnics.

Threading is a little tricky. I've written out in full the threading for the Borders and Motif B with the color scheme above the graph. When I wind the warp, I wind the correct number of colors needed and then break and change the thread. I find this approach easier than grouping the colors to separate later. I also dress my loom from front to back, which allows me to put the colors through the reed in the correct position.

Begin the towel with 3.5 inches (8.9 cm) of Yellow tabby. Then follow the color placement as in the warp: 4 Red tabby, 2 Green tabby, 4 Orange tabby. Next, weave 0.5 inches (1.3 cm) of Yellow tabby, and then weave your first row of popsicles. Now weave 0.5 inches (1.3 cm) of Yellow tabby. Then begin again with the three colors and repeat until you have woven 5 rows of popsicles. Finish with 4 Red, 2 Green, and 4 Orange tabby passes. Finally, weave another 3.5 inches (8.9 cm) of plain weave. Weave 4 passes of a high-contrast thread and weave your second towel.

Note: Be sure to read Chapter 1, "The Most Important Chapter," before beginning any project in this book.

Dimensions: 16.5 × 22 inches (41.9 × 55.9 cm)

Warp
Sett: 20 epi, 10 dent reed, 2 threads per dent
Length: 3-yard (2.7-m) warp
Threads: 8/2 Cotton Clouds Aurora Earth
- Yellow: 252 ends, 800 yards (731.5 m)
- Orange: 30 ends, 100 yards (91.4 m)
- Dark Red: 32 ends (includes 2 floating selvedges), 100 yards (91.4 m)
- Kelly Green: 20 ends, 75 yards (68.6 m)

Weft
8/2 Cotton Clouds Aurora Earth
- Yellow: 525 yards (480 m)
- Dark Red: 55 yards (50.3 m)
- Orange: 55 yards (50.3 m)
- Purple: 30 yards (27.4 m)
- Dark Turk: 30 yards (27.4 m)
- Kelly Green: 15 yards (13.7 m)
- Beige: 100 yards (91.4 m)

Threading
Border: 1 time
Alternate Motifs A and B: 6 times
Motif A: 1 time
Border: 1 time

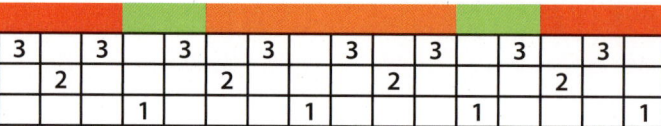

Border
16 ends

Motif B
8 ends

Motif A
36 ends

Tie-up and Treadling

Treadling
Use tabby.

Tabby

Popsicle stick Brown

Popsicle color

36 | FLAVORS OF SUMMER

Lickety-Split

Ice cream—the perfect food! I have yet to find a flavor that I don't like. It is ideal in the summer when it is so hot, and yet I find that eating ice cream in the cold winter is just as enjoyable. These towels would be fun to use if you are having an ice cream party or summer picnic.

Begin your towels with 3.5 inches (8.9 cm) of plain weave in White. Next you will weave your first row of ice cream cones. Now you have a decision to make: What color/flavor for the ice cream? Each of the ice cream cones has two scoops, although you could reduce that to one scoop or increase to three scoops. Since the base color of the towel is White, be sure to use a good contrast color so the ice cream shows well. I used Light Turk for blueberry, Dark Brown for chocolate, Special Pink for strawberry, and Lime Green for mint or pistachio—and, of course, Dark Red for the cherry on top! Weave 1 inch (2.5 cm) of White plain weave between the rows of ice cream cones.

End your towel with 3.5 inches (8.9 cm) of White plain weave. Weave 4 passes of a high-contrast thread to separate the towels, and then weave the second towel. Finish your towels with a rolled hem.

Note: Be sure to read Chapter 1, "The Most Important Chapter," before beginning any project in this book.

Dimensions: 16.5 × 22 inches (41.9 × 55.8 cm)

Warp
Sett: 20 epi, 10 dent reed, 2 threads per dent
Length: 3-yard (2.7-m) warp
Threads: 8/2 Cotton Clouds Aurora Earth
- Mustard: 10 ends (includes 2 floating selvedges), 35 yards (32 m)
- White: 324 ends, 975 yards (891.5 m)

Weft
8/2 Cotton Clouds Aurora Earth
- White: 525 yards (480 m)
- Cones: Mustard, 120 yards (109.7 m)
- Cherries: Dark Red, 40 yards (36.6 m)

Ice cream flavors for a row of one scoop: Light Turk, Dark Brown, Special Pink, Lime Green: approximately 10 yards (9.1 m)

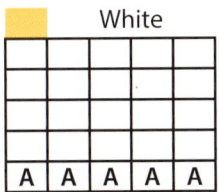

Border 2
20 ends

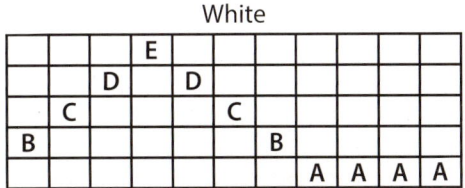

Full Motif
44 ends

Border 1
4 ends

Threading
Border 1: 1 time
Full Motif: 7 times
Border 2: 1 time

Tie-up and Treadling

Treadling
Use tabby.

It's Spicy

I will use this towel when I have a taco party and maybe even create a matching table runner and then decorate with a centerpiece of various types of chili peppers and wow my guests. Of course, not all chili peppers are red as in my towels. You could add some green jalapeño or yellow Corno Di Toro peppers and really make your towel spicy!

Begin your towel with 3.5 inches (8.9 cm) of White plain weave. Next weave 4 passes of Red, 4 passes of White, and 4 passes of Red plain weave. This is the same color sequence as in the threading. Follow this with 0.5 inches (1.3 cm) of White plain weave. Now you will weave your first row of chili peppers, followed by another 0.5 inches (1.3 cm) of White plain weave. Repeat this sequence until you have woven 5 rows of chili peppers. End the last chili pepper row with Red/White/Red sequence. Weave 3.5 inches (8.9 cm) of White plain weave to complete the first towel.

Weave 4 passes of a high-contrast color to separate the towels, and then weave the second towel. Finish your towels with a rolled hem.

Note: Be sure to read Chapter 1, "The Most Important Chapter," before beginning any project in this book.

Dimensions: 16 × 25 inches (40.6 × 63.5 cm)

Warp
Sett: 20 epi, 10 dent reed, 2 threads per dent
Length: 3-yard (2.7-m) warp
Threads: 8/2 Cotton Clouds Aurora Earth
- Dark Red: 66 ends (includes 2 floating selvedges), 225 yards (205.7 m)
- White: 256 ends, 800 yards (731.5 m)

Weft
8/2 Cotton Clouds Aurora Earth
- Dark Red: 250 yards (228.6 m)
- White: 575 yards (525.8 m)
- Kelly Green: 50 yards (45.7 m)

Threading
Full Motif: 7 times
Partial Motif: 1 time

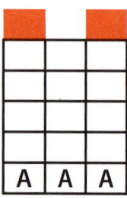

Partial Motif
12 ends

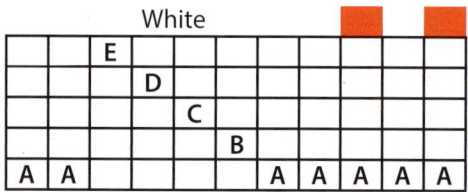

Full Motif
44 ends

Treadling
Use tabby.

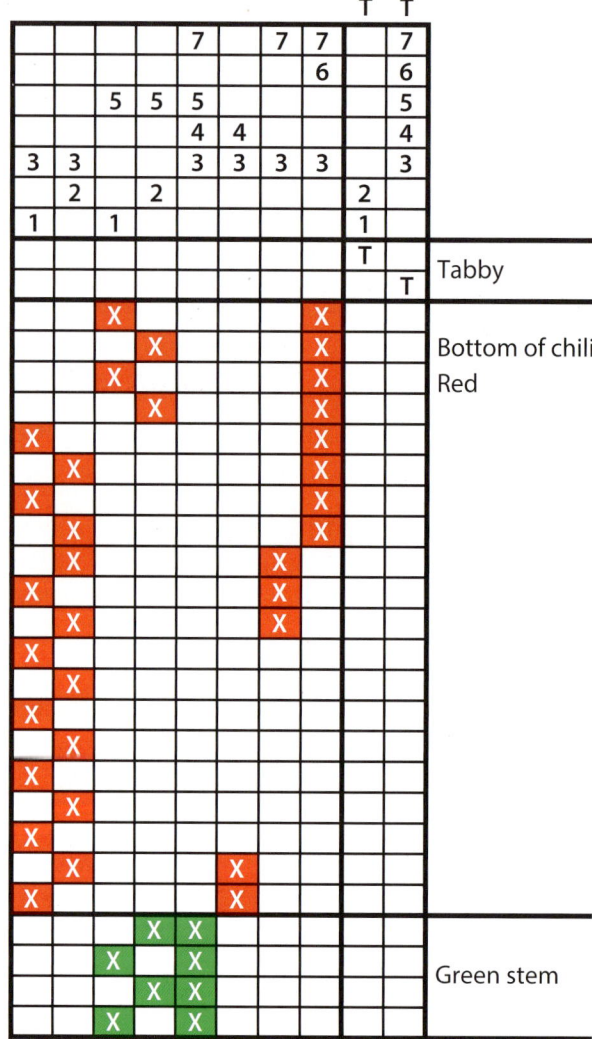

Play Me a Tune

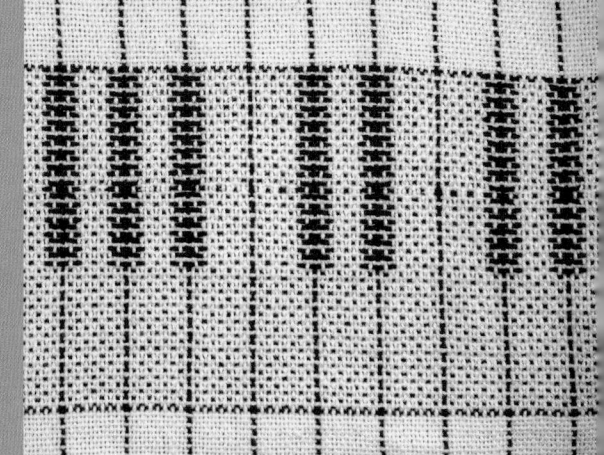

This is the perfect pattern for the pianist! While I decided to make towels, you could use this draft to make scarves, table runners, or placemats. One repeat of the threading completes one octave on the keyboard. Can you find middle C? These towels have three complete octaves.

I used 100% cotton for the towels. But when I make a scarf, I will use Tencel or silk. That will give the keys some shine and the final piece a beautiful drape. For a table runner, I would use perle cotton. I love the sheen of the perle cotton. Just make sure that you use the correct sett for your fiber choice. If you have to add more keys, be sure to keep them in the correct keyboard arrangement.

Now to address the color placement for the warp. Just know that it is consistent throughout the piece: 1 Black–15 White–1 Black–15 White–repeat–end with 1 Black. There is also an additional Black thread on each side, which is your floating selvedge. When I wind my warp, I wind the first color—in this case, 1 Black (plus the floating selvedge, so at the beginning and end there will be two Black threads)—and then cut the thread, tie on White and wind the 15 White warp threads, and so on. This is a slower process, but it does keep the threads in the correct color order.

I dress my loom from front to back, so I have the reed sleyed first and my threads are already in order. It might be a bit more difficult dressing from back to front. Keep in mind that the Black thread will always be threaded on shaft 1. That is a helpful hint.

When treadling this pattern, keep in mind the direction of the motif. For the hem, weave 3.5 inches (8.9 cm) of White plain weave. Then begin the keys by weaving 1 Black thread in plain weave, which outlines the keys. Next weave the White keys followed by the Black keys, ending with 1 Black thread in plain weave. When you get to the end of the project, you will reverse this process, weaving the Black keys first and ending with the White keys. I've included the number of repeats I used for the towels. These may change if you change the size of your threads, so you will have to design as you weave.

In the center of the towel, I wove 3 inches (7.6 cm) of White plain weave and then 1 Black plain weave. This process was repeated four times before beginning the piano keys again. Finish with 3.5 inches (8.9 cm) of White plain weave. Weave 4 passes of a high-contrast color, and then weave your second towel. Finish your towels with a rolled hem.

Note: Be sure to read Chapter 1, "The Most Important Chapter," before beginning any project in this book.

Dimensions: 16.5 × 24 inches (41.9 × 61 cm)

Warp
Sett: 20 epi, 10 dent reed, 2 threads per dent
Length: 3-yard (2.7-m) warp
Threads: 8/2 Cotton Clouds Aurora Earth
- Black: 24 ends (includes 2 floating selvedges), 80 yards (73.2 m)
- White: 315 ends, 975 yards (891.5 m)

Weft
8/2 Cotton Clouds Aurora Earth
- White: 600 yards (548.6 m)
- Black: 75 yards (68.6 m)

Threading
Full Motif: 3 times
Final thread: 1 time
See text for color placement.

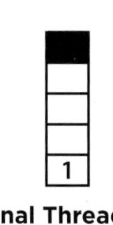

Final Thread to Balance

| | A | A | | B | B | | A | A | | B | B | | A | A | | B | B | | A | A | A | A | A | A | | B | B | | A | A | | B | B | | A | A | A |

Full Motif
112 ends

Tie-up and Treadling

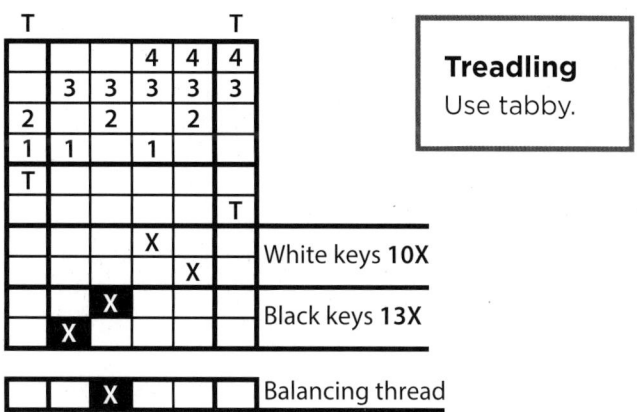

Treadling
Use tabby.

Jack-O'-Lantern

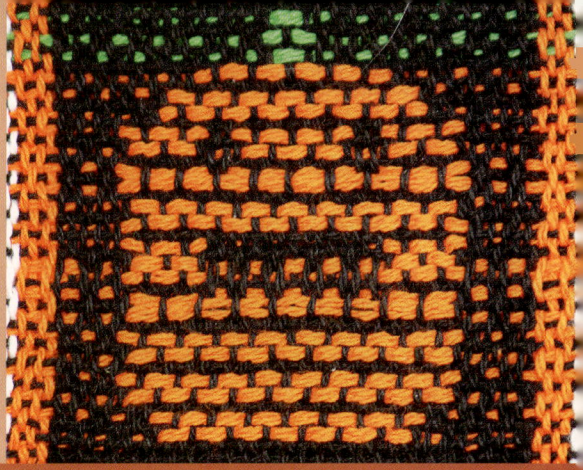

Halloween has become a major holiday, so why not weave some festive towels to add to the decorations? You could choose to weave a table runner or even a scarf with this pattern. For the towels, begin by weaving 3 inches (7.6 cm) of Black plain weave. For Block A, weave 4 passes of Orange, 4 passes of White, and 4 passes of Orange. Follow this with 0.5 inches (1.3 cm) of Black, and then weave the first row of jack-o'-lanterns. Continue with another 0.5 inches (1.3 cm) of Black plain weave, ending with 4 passes of Orange, 4 passes of White, and 4 passes of Orange. Note that to create the tabby, you will have to depress two treadles at a time.

For Block B, weave 1.25 inches (3.2 cm) of Black plain weave. Repeat the stripe sequence: 4 passes Orange, 4 passes White, and 4 passes Orange. Weave another 1.25 inches (3.2 cm) of Black plain weave.

Repeat Block A, followed by Block B, and end with Block A. You will have a total of 3 rows of jack-o'-lanterns for each towel. End with one stripe sequence. Finish the towel with 3 inches (7.6 cm) of Black plain weave.

Weave 4 passes of a high-contrast color, and then weave the second towel. Finish each towel with a rolled hem.

Note: Be sure to read Chapter 1, "The Most Important Chapter," before beginning any project in this book.

Dimensions: 16.5 × 23 inches (41.9 × 58.4 cm)

Warp
Sett: 20 epi, 10 dent reed, 2 threads per dent
Length: 3-yard (2.7-m) warp
Threads: 8/2 Cotton Clouds Aurora Earth
- Orange: 50 ends (includes 2 floating selvedges), 175 yards (160 m)
- Black: 260 ends, 800 yards (731.5 m)
- White: 24 ends, 100 yards (91.4 m)

Weft
8/2 Cotton Clouds Aurora Earth
- Black: 600 yards (548.6 m)
- Orange: 175 yards (160 m)
- White: 30 yards (27.4 m)
- Winter Green: 25 yards (22.9 m)

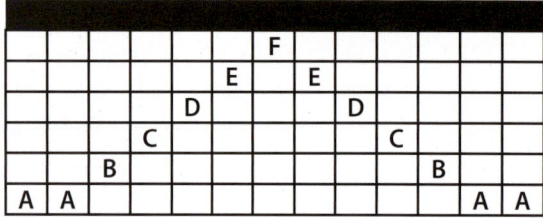
Block B
52 ends

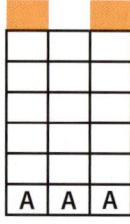
Block A
12 ends

Threading
Alternate Blocks A and B: 5 times
Block A: 1 time

Tie-up and Treadling

Treadling
Use tabby.

Tabby
Base of pumpkin
Top of pumpkin
Stem

48 | JACK-O'-LANTERN

Autumn Leaves

Beginning in September, my color palette changes from greens to browns, rusts, and golds. I like to start using towels woven in these colors. This set of towels will be a favorite in my kitchen. It would be easy to change the width and length and create a matching table runner. Wouldn't that be wonderful for Thanksgiving?

Begin the towel with 3 inches (7.6 cm) of plain weave in Natural. Then you will start weaving rows of leaves. For one towel, I used only one color for each row of leaves. But for the second towel I got more creative. Since I was using 8/2 cotton instead of 4/8 cotton, I was able to put two colors into each shed. This approach required using three shuttles. I used all of the colors listed in no particular order. Combining the colors in this way allows the leaves to have a soft, blended color palette. Either way is wonderful, and you will get to choose. You could use different colors of green and make a set of towels that is more springlike.

Weave 0.5 inches (1.3 cm) of plain weave between each row of leaves. After you have woven 9 rows, weave another 3 inches (7.6 cm) of plain weave in Natural. Then weave 4 passes of a high-contrast color and weave your second towel. Finish each towel with a rolled hem.

Note: Be sure to read Chapter 1, "The Most Important Chapter," before beginning any project in this book.

Dimensions: 16.5 × 24.5 inches (41.9 × 62.2 cm)

Warp
Sett: 20 epi, 10 dent reed, 2 threads per dent
Length: 3-yard (2.7-m) warp
Threads: 8/2 Cotton Clouds Aurora Earth
- Rust: 10 ends (includes 2 floating selvedges), 35 yards (32 m)
- Natural: 324 ends, 980 yards (896.1 m)

Weft
8/2 Cotton Clouds Aurora Earth
Plain weave and tabby: Natural, 575 yards (525.8 m)
Per leaf (9 leaves per towel):
- Stem: 6 yards (5.5 m)
- Leaf: 15 yards (13.7 m)

If using two colors for leaves and 8/2 cotton: 7.5 yards (6.9 m) of each color for *each* leaf
Colors: Rust, Gold, Dark Green, Loden Green, Light Orange, Light Brown, Chocolate, Wine

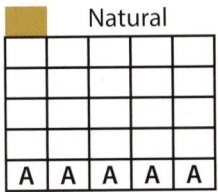
Border 2
20 ends

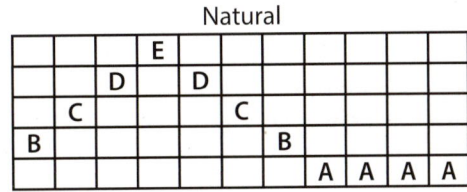
Full Motif
44 ends

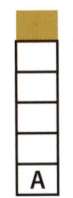
Border 1
4 ends

Threading
Border 1: 1 time
Full Motif: 7 times
Border 2: 1 time

Tie-up and Treadling

Treadling
Use tabby.

AUTUMN LEAVES | 51

Pumpkin Patch

While this pattern makes some wonderful dish towels, it would also make a fantastic table runner for the fall season. These pumpkins are easy to weave. I used only Orange for the pumpkins, but you could use many different colors. Just check out your farmer's market for ideas.

For the warp, there were three colors used. The narrow vertical stripes are Dark Green. Motif B alternates colors. The layout of the colors is as follows:

Natural–Polo Tan–Champagne–Natural–Champagne–Polo Tan–Natural

Begin the towel with 3 inches (7.6 cm) of plain weave in Natural. Then weave 4 passes of the Dark Green tabby. Following the layout of the colors in the warp, weave 0.5 inches (1.3 cm) of plain weave, followed by the first row of pumpkins and 0.5 inches (1.3 cm) of plain weave. A Dark Green stripe of 4 passes will separate each row of pumpkins. Use the next warp color for the next block, and so on. If changing the colors in the weft is confusing, you can use just one color of your choice. You will weave a total of 8 rows of pumpkins.

After the last row of pumpkins, weave 4 passes of plain weave in Dark Green and then 3 inches (7.6 cm) of plain weave in Natural. Weave 4 passes of a high-contrast color to separate the towels, and then weave your second towel. Finish the towels with a rolled hem.

Note: Be sure to read Chapter 1, "The Most Important Chapter," before beginning any project in this book.

Dimensions: 17 × 26 inches (43.2 × 66 cm)

Warp
Sett: 20 epi, 10 dent reed, 2 threads per dent
Length: 3-yard (2.7-m) warp
Threads: 8/2 Cotton Clouds Aurora Earth
- Natural: 132 ends, 425 yards (388.6 m)
- Champagne: 88 ends, 275 yards (251.5 m)
- Polo Tan: 88 ends, 275 yards (251.5 m)
- Dark Green: 34 ends (includes 2 floating selvedges), 110 yards (100.6 m)

Weft
8/2 Cotton Clouds Aurora Earth
- Natural: 250 yards (228.6 m)
- Champagne: 180 yards (164.6 m)
- Polo Tan: 180 yards (164.6 m)
- Dark Green: 80 yards (73.2 m)

Pattern thread: 8/2 Cotton Clouds Aurora Earth
- Orange: 250 yards (228.6 m)
- Dark Green: 75 yards (68.6 m)

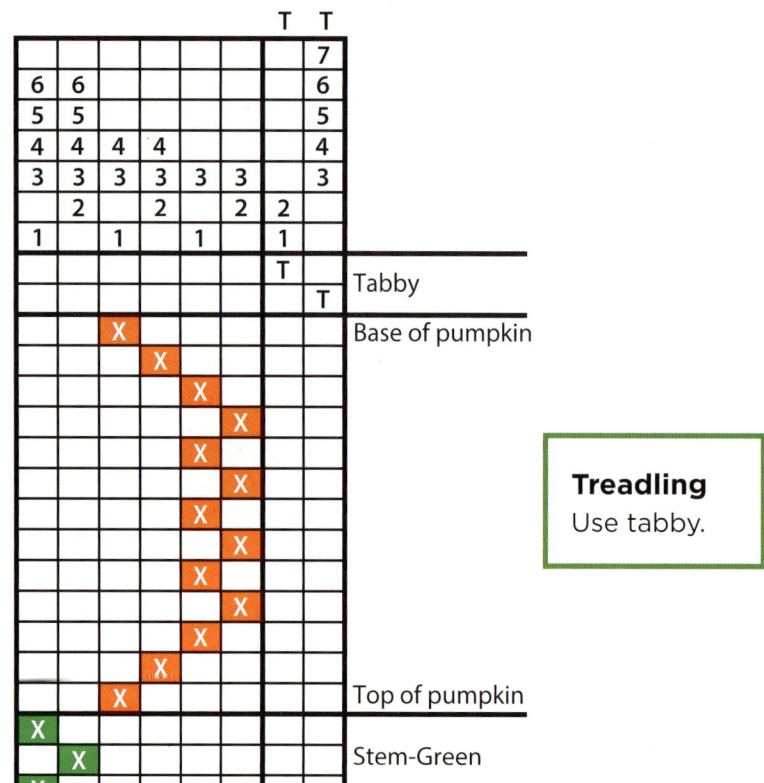

Three Crosses

In the narthex of our church, there is a long table that holds flowers and other small items—a very welcoming sight for members and visitors. This runner will be a wonderful addition to that table. It was woven in gold tones, but you could think about colors used for various religious holidays and weave a series of runners in different colors. Change the width and/or length to fit whatever table you will be using it on.

Begin by weaving 8 inches (20.3 cm) in the background pattern, and yes, you will be depressing two treadles at a time. This method creates a lovely pattern throughout your runner. Then the motif is woven one time using the tabby after each pattern thread. Repeat the background pattern for 31 inches (78.7 cm) or as desired. Then repeat the motif, but be sure to reverse the pattern. Finish with another 8 inches (20.3 cm) of background pattern. I finished the runner with a rolled hem, but you could also leave a fringe. This runner is lovely on both sides.

Note: Be sure to read Chapter 1, "The Most Important Chapter," before beginning any project in this book.

Dimensions: 13 × 48 inches (33 × 121.9 cm)

Warp
Sett: 24 epi, 12 dent reed, 2 threads per dent
Length: 2.5-yard (2.3-m) warp
10/2 Yarn Barn Cotton
- California Gold: 171 ends (includes 2 floating selvedges), 450 yards (411.5 m)
- White: 148 ends, 400 yards (365.8 m)

Weft
5/2 Yarn Barn Cotton: California Gold, 400 yards (365.8 m)
Tabby: 10/2 Yarn Barn Cotton: White, 400 yards (365.8 m)

Balancing Motif
1 end

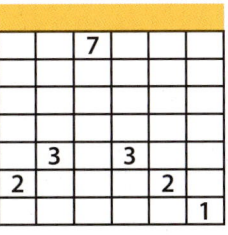

Motif A
6 ends

> **Threading**
> Motif A: 14 times
> Center Section: 1 time
> Motif A: 14 times
> Balancing Motif: 1 time

White

									E	E	E																		
							D	D	D				D	D	D														
			C	C																				C	C				
	B	B			B	B															B	B				B	B		
A	A	A	A					A	A	A	A					A	A	A	A									A	A	A	A

Center Section
148 ends

Tie-up and Treadling

Treadling
Use tabby.

					T	T	
						7	
		6	6	6	6	6	
5	5					5	
4	4	4	4			4	
3	3	3	3	3	3	3	
	2		2		2	2	
1		1		1		1	
					T		Tabby
						T	
				X		X	Background
					X	X	pattern
					X	X	
				X		X	
X				X			Beg. of cross
	X				X		Vertical beam of
X				X			center cross **1X**
	X				X		
		X					Vertical beams of
			X				3 crosses **7X**
			X				
		X			X		Horizontal beams of
			X				small crosses **1X**
		X			X		
			X				
		X					Vertical beam finishes
			X				small crosses **1X**
		X					
			X				
X							
	X						Horizontal beam of
X							large center cross
	X						**1X**
X							
	X						
X			X				
	X			X			
X			X				Top of cross
	X			X			Vertical beam of
X			X				center cross **1X**
	X			X			

Scary Skulls

Halloween wouldn't be the same without a skeleton or two. This set of towels really fits into the season, and you can pair them up with the Jack-O'-Lantern towels. Feel free to decrease the number of skulls. You could add horizontal stripes if you like that look better. This pattern would also make a fun scarf for the season. For a scarf, I would suggest working three motifs wide and just one motif at each end and weaving in perle cotton or Tencel. Add some fancy beads to the fringe!

For these towels, weave 3.5 inches (8.9 cm) of Black plain weave. Then weave the first row of skulls. Each skull measures approximately 2 inches (5.1 cm), so if you want to make changes, this will help you to decide what you would like to do. There are 2 inches (5.1 cm) of Black plain weave between each row of skulls and a total of 6 rows of skulls. Finish with another 3.5 inches (8.9 cm) plain weave at the end of each towel. Weave 4 passes of a high-contrast color, and then weave the second towel. Finish your towels with a rolled hem.

Note: Be sure to read Chapter 1, "The Most Important Chapter," before beginning any project in this book.

Dimensions: 16.5 × 26 inches (41.9 × 66 cm)

Warp
Sett: 20 epi, 10 dent reed, 2 threads per dent
Length: 3-yard (2.7-m) warp
Threads: 8/2 Cotton Clouds Aurora Earth
- Black: 260 ends, 800 yards (731.5 m)
- White: 24 ends, 80 yards (73.2 m)
- Orange: 50 ends (includes 2 floating selvedges), 175 yards (160 m)

Weft
8/2 Cotton Clouds Aurora Earth
- Black: 600 yards (548.6 m)
- White: 300 yards (274.3 m)

Motif B
52 ends

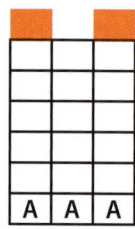

Motif A
12 ends

Threading
Alternate Motifs A and B: 5 times
Motif A: 1 time

Tie-up and Treadling

Treadling
Use tabby.

T									T	
							8	8	8	
								7	7	
					6	6			6	
					5	5			5	
		4	4					4	4	
		3	3	3	3	3	3	3	3	
2		2		2		2				
1	1		1		1					
T									T	Tabby
	X									
		X								Bottom of head
	X									
		X								
			X					X		
				X				X		Mouth
			X					X		
			X							
			X							
				X						
			X			X				
				X			X			Nose
			X			X				
			X							Bridge
			X							
					X					
				X						Eyes
					X					
			X							
			X							
		X								
	X									Top of head

Dog Tales

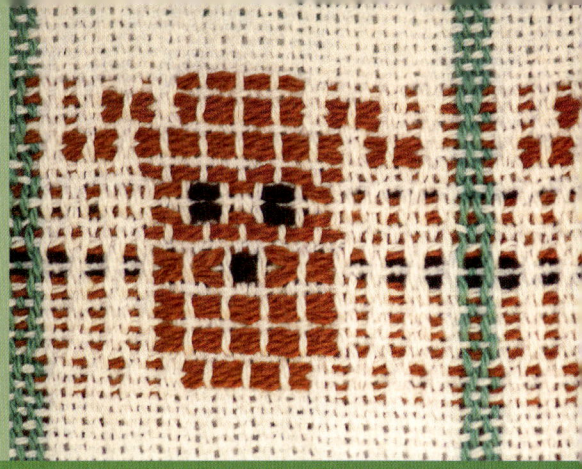

This is for all of you dog lovers! However, this canine is just a mutt, which is always my favorite breed. I used three different browns, so all of my dogs look a bit different. If you have a light-colored dog, just change the color of the background to make your dog stand out. You can easily change the color of the eyes as well.

When reading the treadling, be sure to notice that when weaving the eyes and nose, you will be placing two colors before throwing the tabby. This approach compacts the threads and makes the eyes and nose more prominent. Just take your time through this section. The tabby thread is always White for this set of towels.

Weave 4 inches (10.2 cm) of Aqua plain weave, followed by 0.5 inches (1.3 cm) of White plain weave. Then weave your first row of dogs. Follow with 0.5 inches (1.3 cm) of White plain weave. Repeat this until you have 7 rows of dogs. Then finish with 4 inches (10.2 cm) of Aqua plain weave. Weave 4 passes of a high-contrast color, and then weave your second towel. Finish the towels with a rolled hem.

Note: Be sure to read Chapter 1, "The Most Important Chapter," before beginning any project in this book.

Dimensions: 17 × 25 inches (43.2 × 63.5 cm)

Warp
- **Sett:** 20 epi, 10 dent reed, 2 threads per dent
- **Length:** 3-yard (2.7-m) warp
- **Threads:** 8/2 Cotton Clouds Aurora Earth
  - White: 308 ends, 950 yards (868.7 m)
  - Aqua: 34 ends (includes 2 floating selvedges), 115 yards (105.2 m)

Weft
8/2 Cotton Clouds Aurora Earth
- White: 600 yards (548.6 m)
- Aqua: 200 yards (182.9 m)
- Light Brown: 250 yards (228.6 m)
- Cinnamon: 200 yards (182.9 m)
- Rust: 200 yards (182.9 m)
- Black: 70 yards (64 m)

White

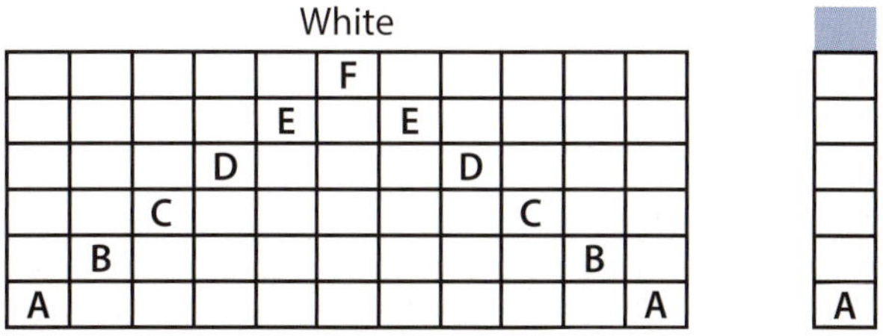

				F					
			E		E				
		D				D			
	C						C		
B								B	
A									A

Motif B
44 ends

A

Motif A
4 ends

Tie-up and Treadling

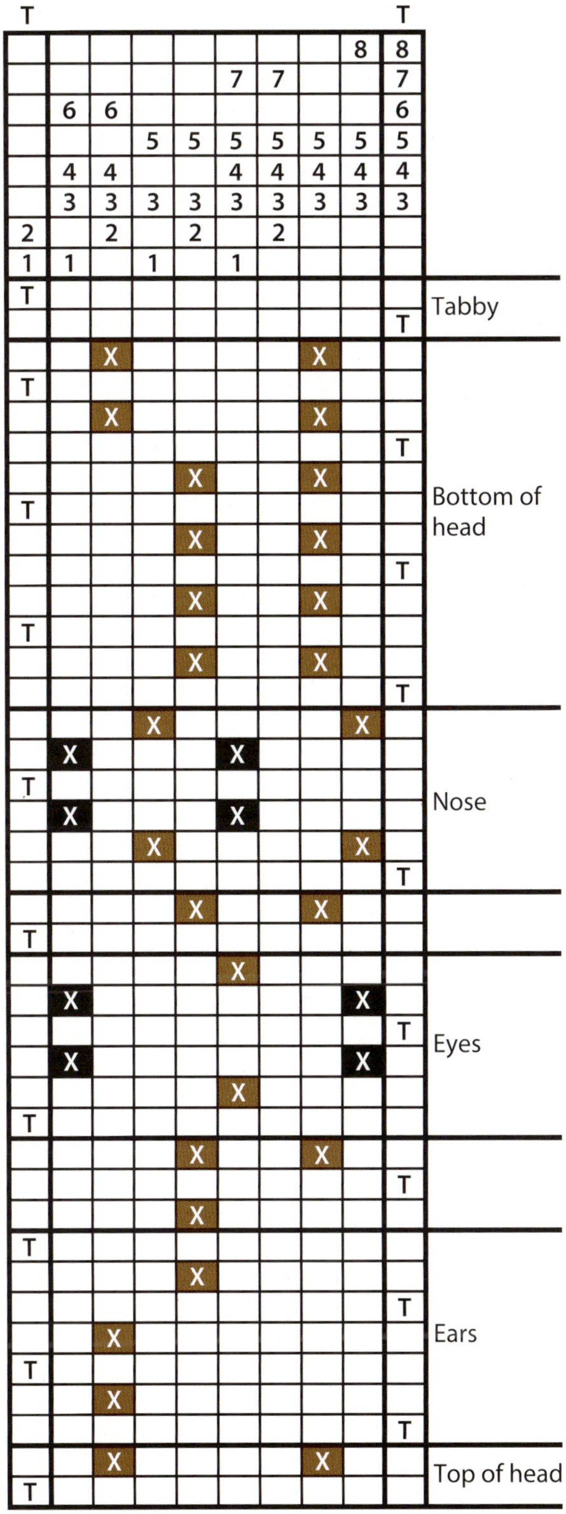

Threading
Alternate Motifs A and B: 7 times
Motif A: 1 time

Treadling
Insert tabby as indicated.

Labels on treadling (top to bottom): Tabby, Bottom of head, Nose, Eyes, Ears, Top of head

DOG TALES | 63

There's No Place Like Gnome

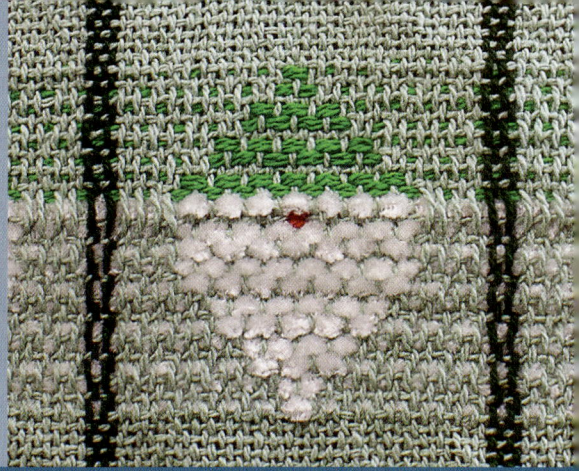

Garden gnomes are oh, so popular. This image brings gnomes into the home, whether you make a set of towels or a runner for your table. There are six rows of gnomes on each towel and three colors of hats. You could use six different colors for hats if you like. This would be a great way to use up some of those small amounts of fiber that we all have.

Begin with 3.5 inches (8.9 cm) of plain weave in Nile Green and then 4 passes of Dark Green. Follow with 0.5 inches (1.3 cm) of Nile Green, and then weave your first row of gnomes.

When you get to the nose section, you will notice that the tabby is *after* two sets of pattern threads. *This is correct.* Just follow the treadling pattern, and all will work out. The tabby color throughout the towels is Nile Green.

After you have woven your first row of gnomes, weave 0.5 inches (1.3 cm) of plain weave and then 4 passes of Dark Green. Repeat until you have woven six rows of gnomes. Follow the last row with 4 passes of Dark Green and another 3.5 inches (8.9 cm) of plain weave in Nile Green. Weave 4 passes of a high-contrast color to separate the towels, and then weave your second towel. Finish each towel with a rolled hem.

Can you substitute cotton for the chenille? Yes, you can, but you might not be happy with the result. You will not have the fuzzy beard, which really makes such a cute gnome. Plus, neither 8/2 cotton nor 4/8 cotton will cover as well, and the beard will look thinner. Treat the chenille just as you would 8/2 cotton. Place two threads in one dent for your pattern thread.

Note: Be sure to read Chapter 1, "The Most Important Chapter," before beginning any project in this book.

Dimensions: 17 × 25 inches (43.2 × 63.5 cm)

Warp
Sett: 20 epi, 10 dent reed, 2 threads per dent
Length: 3-yard (2.7-m) warp
Threads: 8/2 Cotton Clouds Aurora Earth
- Nile Green: 308 ends, 950 yards (868.7 m)
- Dark Green: 34 ends (includes 2 floating selvedges), 125 yards (114.3 m)

Weft
8/2 Cotton Clouds Aurora Earth
- Nile Green: 600 yards (548.6 m)
- Dark Green: 50 yards (45.7 m)
- Dark Red: 100 yards (91.4 m)
- Blue: 100 yards (91.4 m)
- Kelly Green: 100 yards (91.4 m)
- Dark Red (nose): 30 yards (27.4 m)
Maurice Brassard 8/2 White Chenille: 150 yards (137.2 m)

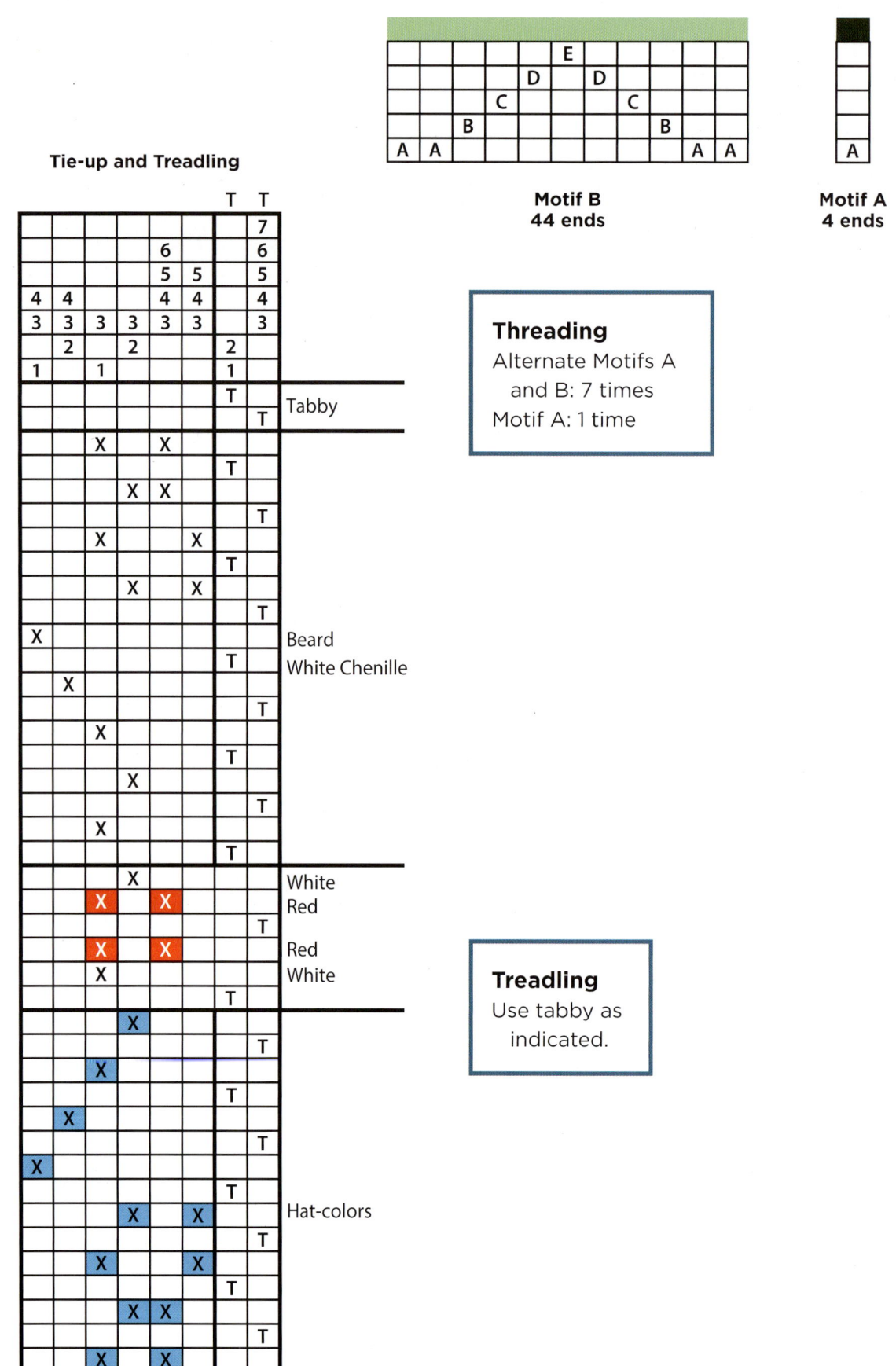

Santa Claus

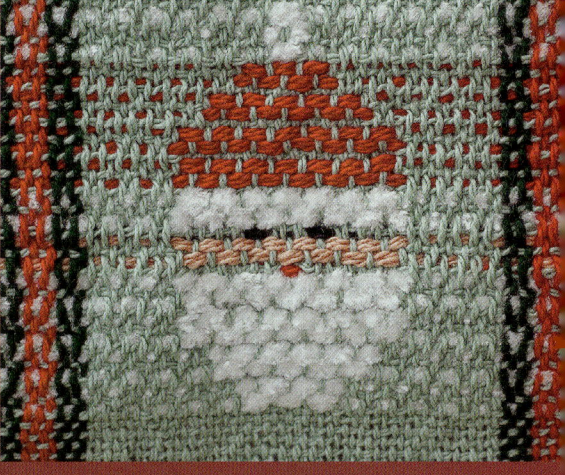

This set of towels really gets you in the mood for the holidays! It would also be a cute table runner! I used chenille for the beard so that the image really has some texture.

Begin the towel with 3.5 inches (8.9 cm) of plain weave using the Nile Green. Now you will weave your first row of Santas. *It is very important that you use the 1-2 tabby after the first pattern thread.* If you don't, your image will not look correct! Also follow the tabby placement as indicated in the face section of the draft. Yes, you will be putting two colors in before you add the tabby. Once again, this is very important to allow the face to be correct. Just take your time working through the face—don't be in a hurry!

After you finish your first row of Santas, weave 1.5 inches (3.8 cm) of plain weave. Repeat this pattern until you have woven 6 rows of Santa faces. End the towel with another 3.5 inches (8.9 cm) of plain weave. Weave 4 passes of a high-contrast color, and then weave the second towel. Finish each towel with a rolled hem.

Note: Be sure to read Chapter 1, "The Most Important Chapter," before beginning any project in this book.

Dimensions: 16.5 × 25 inches (41.9 × 63.5 cm)

Warp
Sett: 20 epi, 10 dent reed, 2 threads per dent
Length: 3-yard (2.7-m) warp
Threads: 8/2 Cotton Clouds Aurora Earth
- Nile Green: 260 ends, 800 yards (731.5 m)
- Dark Red: 24 ends, 80 yards (73.2 m)
- Dark Green: 50 ends (includes 2 floating selvedges), 175 yards (160 m)

Weft
8/2 Cotton Clouds Aurora Earth
- Nile Green: 575 yards (525.8 m)
- Dark Red: 125 yards (114.3 m)
- Black: 20 yards (18.3 m)
- Peach: 35 yards (32 m)

Maurice Brassard White Chenille: 175 yards (160 m)

Tie-up and Treadling

- Tabby
- Beard — White Chenille
- White Chenille
- Nose-Red
- Flesh
- Flesh
- Eyes-Black
- Hat Fur — White Chenille
- Hat — Red
- Pom-pom — White Chenille

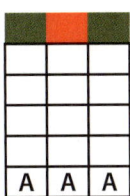

Motif A
12 ends

Motif B
52 ends

Threading

Alternate Motifs A and B: 5 times
Motif A: 1 time

Treadling

Use tabby as indicated.

SANTA CLAUS | 69

Southwest Sunset

This set is for Jodi, the owner of Cotton Clouds, who makes such beautiful yarn kits for many of my patterns! Living in the Southwest encompasses a whole new color palette. Sunset and sunrise are particularly beautiful, as the reds, oranges, and yellows are so vibrant. These cacti are woven in two different manners. On one towel, the cacti are created with only one color: Dark Green. On the second towel, the cacti are woven using Dark Green and Peridot variegated cotton. You have a choice as to which look you like the best. When I used the combination of Dark Green and Peridot, I used three shuttles: one shuttle for the Dark Green, one shuttle for the Peridot, and one shuttle for the tabby.

What follows is the color sequence for the warp:

Light Orange–Maize–Cinnamon–Maize–Light Orange

Begin with 3.5 inches (8.9 cm) of plain weave in Cinnamon. Follow the color placement of the warp for the sequence of the tabby thread. Weave 0.75 inches (1.9 cm) of plain weave, and then weave the first row of cacti. End the pattern block with another 0.75 inches (1.9 cm) of plain weave. You will weave a total of 5 rows of cacti. End with 3.5 inches (8.9 cm) of plain weave in Cinnamon. Weave 4 passes of a high-contrast color, and then weave the second towel. Finish the towels with a rolled hem.

Note: Be sure to read Chapter 1, "The Most Important Chapter," before beginning any project in this book.

Dimensions: 17 × 26 inches (43.2 × 66 cm)

Warp
Sett: 20 epi, 10 dent reed, 2 threads per dent
Length: 3-yard (2.7-m) warp
Threads: 8/2 Cotton Clouds Aurora Earth
- Light Orange: 138 ends (includes 2 floating selvedges), 450 yards (411.5 m)
- Maize: 136 ends, 450 yards (411.5 m)
- Cinnamon: 68 ends, 225 yards (205.7 m)

Weft
8/2 Cotton Clouds Aurora Earth
- Cinnamon: 250 yards (228.6 m)
- Light Orange: 200 yards (182.9 m)
- Maize: 200 yards (182.9 m)

If all of the cacti are one color for both towels:
8/2 Cotton Clouds Aurora Earth: Dark Green, 300 yards (274.3 m)

If cacti are Dark Green and variegated fiber:
8/2 Cotton Clouds Aurora Earth
- Dark Green: 150 yards (137.2 m)
- Peridot: 150 yards (137.2 m)

Threading

Repeat Motif 5 times following the color placement indicated in the text.

							F							
						E		E						
					D				D					
				C						C				
			B								B			
A	A	A										A	A	A

Motif
68 ends

Tie-up and Treadling

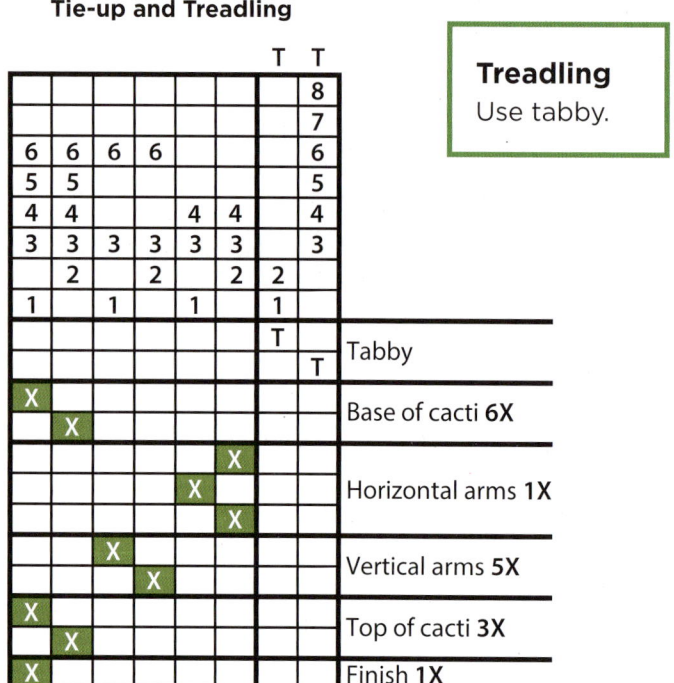

Treadling

Use tabby.

Desert Landscape

Another set for Jodi! But in this set we are looking more at the daytime colors in the Southwest. These towels use browns, cinnamons, and taupes—all the colors we see in the desert. However, the cacti have bloomed and now have fruit. Below is the color sequence for the warp:

Cinnamon–Champagne–Rust–Champagne–Cinnamon

The cacti for this set are woven with Winter Green, and the fruit is woven with Dark Red.

Begin with 3.5 inches (8.9 cm) of plain weave in Cinnamon. Follow the color arrangement below for the tabby blocks:

Champagne–Cinnamon–Rust–Cinnamon–Champagne

Begin each cacti block with 0.75 inches (1.9 cm) of plain weave, and then begin the first row of cacti. End each row with another 0.75 inches (1.9 cm) of plain weave. Repeat this sequence for each cacti row. You will weave a total of 5 rows of cacti following the tabby color sequence above. End the towel with 3.5 inches (8.9 cm) of plain weave in Cinnamon. Weave 4 passes of a high-contrast color, and then weave the second towel. Finish the towels with a rolled hem.

Note: Be sure to read Chapter 1, "The Most Important Chapter," before beginning any project in this book.

Dimensions: 17 × 26 inches (43.2 × 66 cm)

Warp
Sett: 20 epi, 10 dent reed, 2 threads per dent
Length: 3-yard (2.7-m) warp
Threads: 8/2 Cotton Clouds Aurora Earth
- Cinnamon: 138 ends (includes 2 floating selvedges), 450 yards (411.5 m)
- Champagne: 136 ends, 450 yards (411.5 m)
- Rust: 68 ends, 225 yards (205.7 m)

Weft
8/2 Cotton Clouds Aurora Earth
- Cinnamon: 250 yards (228.6 m)
- Rust: 200 yards (182.9 m)
- Champagne: 200 yards (182.9 m)

For the cacti: 8/2 Cotton Clouds Aurora Earth
- Winter Green: 300 yards (274.3 m)
- Dark Red: 75 yards (68.6 m)

Threading

Repeat Motif 5 times following the color placement indicated in the text.

							F						
						E		E					
					D				D				
				C						C			
			B								B		
A	A	A										A	A	A	A

Motif
68 ends

Tie-up and Treadling

Treadling
Use tabby.

Base of cacti	**6X**
Horizontal arms	**1X**
Vertical arms	**5X**
Top of cacti	**3X**
Finish	**1X**
Fruit-Red	**1X**

Just a Green Garden Snake

Many years ago, our daughter worked at a local zoo called Reptiland. The name is self-explanatory. While there, she became a certified venomous snake handler. OK, not my cup of tea, but she loved it. She now raises African sand snakes, and she swears they are very cute. I have come to realize that there are a lot of individuals who love snakes and have them as pets, so this set of towels is for them. Feel free to change the colors as you wish. Or you might just want to call them worms.

The treadling is rather lengthy, and I've given you the tabby position for the head portion. You should notice that in one section there is both a Kelly Green thread and a Black thread for the eyes before the next tabby is thrown. This is very important. Once you get past the eyes, just continue alternating the tabby thread.

There are three sections to the body. Treadle as follows after finishing the head: A–B–A–C.

Repeat this sequence two times and then begin the tail section.

Weave 4 inches (10.2 cm) of plain weave, and then reverse the snake. (Be sure to read the section in Chapter 3 on how to reverse the pattern.)

After you have woven the second snake, weave 3.5 inches (8.9 cm) of plain weave. Then weave 4 passes of a high-contrast color and weave your second towel.

Note: Be sure to read Chapter 1, "The Most Important Chapter," before beginning any project in this book.

Dimensions: 16.5 × 23.5 inches (41.9 × 59.7 cm)

Warp
Sett: 20 epi, 10 dent reed, 2 threads per dent
Length: 3-yard (2.7-m) warp
Threads: 8/2 Cotton Clouds Aurora Earth
- Champagne: 176 ends, 550 yards (502.9 m)
- Natural: 132 ends, 400 yards (365.8 m)
- Kelly Green: 26 ends (includes 2 floating selvedges), 90 yards (82.3 m)

Weft
8/2 Cotton Clouds Aurora Earth
- Natural: 550 yards (502.9 m)
- Kelly Green: 300 yards (274.3 m)
- Dark Red: 75 yards (68.6 m)
- Black: 5 yards (4.6 m)

Natural

Motif B
44 ends

Champagne

Motif A
44 ends

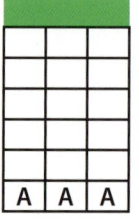

Border
12 ends

Threading

Border: 1 time
Alternate
  Motifs A and
  B: 3 times
Motif A: 1 time
Border: 1 time

Tie-up and Treadling

Treadling sections (left draft, green):
- Tabby
- Head
- Body A
- Body B
- Body C
- Tail
- End

Treadling sections (right draft):
- Tabby
- Begin
- Forked tongue Red
- Straight tongue Red
- Head Green
- Green Eyes Black

Treadling

Tabby is indicated throughout the treadling of the head only. Continue alternating the tabby for the entire snake. *Be sure to read text.*

78 | JUST A GREEN GARDEN SNAKE

Rattlesnake

This is another one for all those reptile lovers. Again, the treadling can be tedious, but it is worth the time. Because this is a venomous snake, its head is more triangular. Begin by weaving 3 inches (7.6 cm) of plain weave. I have given you the tabby position for the head portion. You should notice that in one section there is a Cinnamon thread and a Black thread for the eyes before the next tabby is thrown. This is very important. Once you get past the eyes, just continue alternating the tabby thread.

There are three sections to the body. Treadle as follows after finishing the head: A–B–A–C. And be sure to follow the colorway indicated in the treadling pattern.

Repeat this sequence two times and then begin the tail section. You will end with the Medium Brown for the rattles.

Weave 3.5 inches (8.9 cm) of plain weave, and then reverse the snake. Be sure to read the section in Chapter 3 on how to reverse the pattern. After you have woven the second snake, weave 3 inches (7.6 cm) of plain weave. Then weave 4 passes of a high-contrast color and weave the second towel. Finish each towel with rolled hems.

Note: Be sure to read Chapter 1, "The Most Important Chapter," before beginning any project in this book.

Dimensions: 16.5 × 23.5 inches (41.9 × 59.7 cm)

Warp
Sett: 20 epi, 10 dent reed, 2 threads per dent
Length: 3-yard (2.7-m) warp
Threads: 8/2 Cotton Clouds Aurora Earth
- Nile Green: 176 ends, 550 yards (502.9 m)
- Natural: 132 ends, 400 yards (365.8 m)
- Dark Green: 26 ends (includes 2 floating selvedges), 90 yards (82.3 m)

Weft
8/2 Cotton Clouds Aurora Earth
- Natural: 550 yards (502.9 m)
- Cinnamon: 175 yards (160 m)
- Light Brown: 150 yards (137.2 m)
- Dark Red: 75 yards (68.6 m)
- Black: 5 yards (4.6 m)

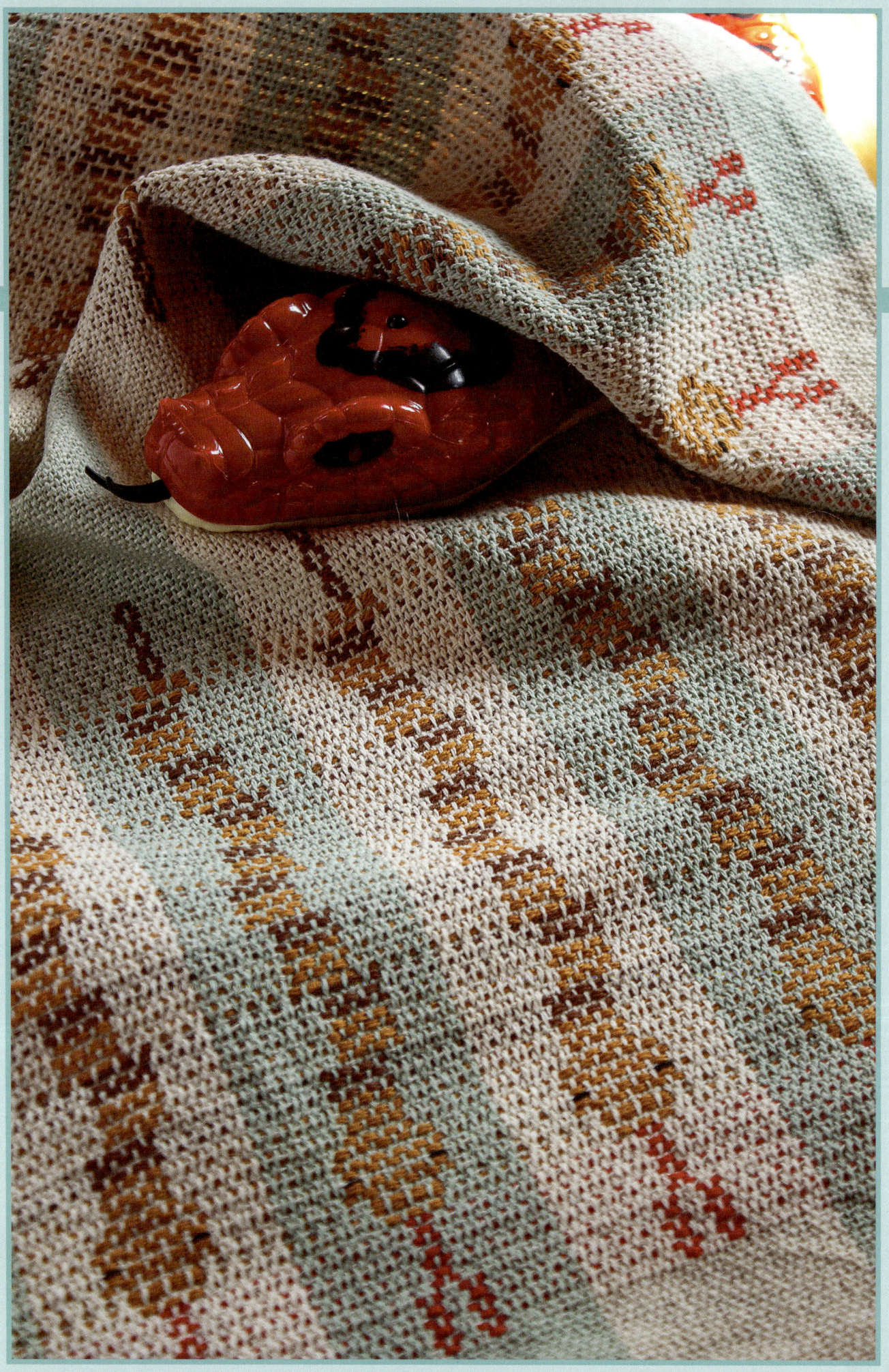

Natural

Motif B
44 ends

Nile Green

Motif A
44 ends

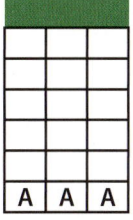

Border
12 ends

Tie-up and Treadling

Tabby
Head
Body A
Body B
Body C
Tail
Rattle 3X
End

Begin
Forked tongue Red
Straight tongue Red
Head
Eyes Black

Threading
Border 1: 1 time
Alternate
  Motifs A and
  B: 3 times
Motif A: 1 time
Border: 1 time

Treadling
Tabby is indicated throughout the treadling of the head only. Continue alternating tabby for the entire snake. *Be sure to read text.*

RATTLESNAKE | 81

Umbrellas for a Rainy Day

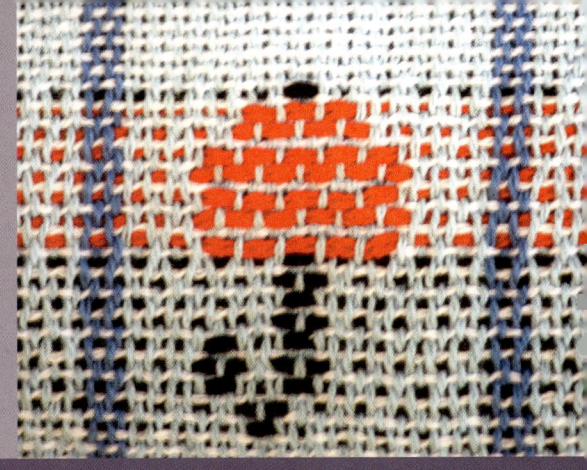

A "just for fun" pattern! It could easily be made into baby shower table decorations, which could later be used as burp cloths by the new mother. Or how about for a wedding shower with the wedding colors and then given to the bride as a gift? These umbrellas are easy to weave, so be sure to give them a try.

Begin with 4 inches (10.2 cm) of White plain weave. I use the White to lighten the blue. Doing so allows the umbrellas to stand out more.

Next weave 4 passes of blue followed by 0.5 inches (1.3 cm) of White tabby. Now you will weave your first row of umbrellas. Finish with another 0.5 inches (1.3 cm) of White tabby and 4 passes of Blue. Repeat this process until you have finished 7 rows of umbrellas. After the last 0.5 inches (1.3 cm) of White tabby, weave 4 passes of Blue, followed by another 4 inches (10.2 cm) of White. Weave 4 passes of a high-contrast color to separate the towels, and then weave the second towel. Finish both towels with rolled hems.

Note: Be sure to read Chapter 1, "The Most Important Chapter," before beginning any project in this book.

Dimensions: 16.5 × 25.5 inches (41.9 × 64.8 cm)

Warp
Sett: 20 epi, 10 dent reed, 2 threads per dent
Length: 3-yard (2.7-m) warp
Threads: 8/2 Cotton Clouds Aurora Earth
- Baby Blue: 288 ends, 875 yards (800.1 m)
- Blue: 46 ends (includes 2 floating selvedges), 150 yards (137.2 m)

Weft
8/2 Cotton Clouds Aurora Earth
- Black: 150 yards (137.2 m)
- Dark Red: 20 yards (18.3 m)
- Turk: 20 yards (18.3 m)
- Purple: 20 yards (18.3 m)
- Orange: 20 yards (18.3 m)
- Kelly Green: 20 yards (18.3 m)
- Rose Red: 20 yards (18.3 m)

Tabby: 8/2 Cotton Clouds Aurora Earth: White, 550 yards (502.9 m)

Threading
Border: 1 time
Alternate Motifs A
  and B: 7 times
Motif A: 1 time
Border: 1 time

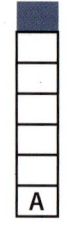

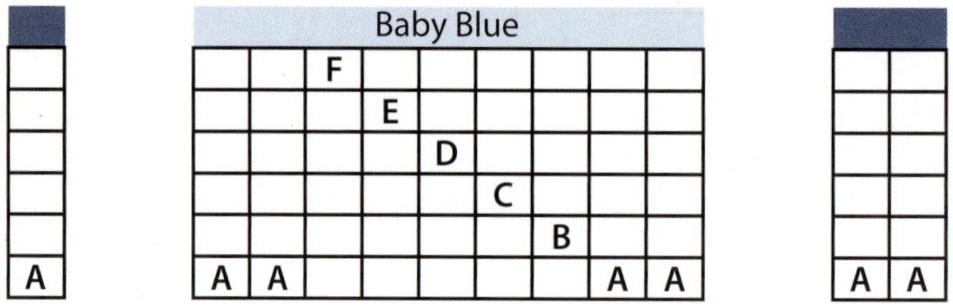

Motif B
4 ends

Baby Blue

		F						
			E					
				D				
					C			
						B		
A	A						A	A

Motif A
36 ends

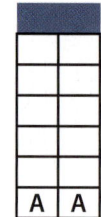

Border
8 ends

Treadling
Use tabby.

Tie-up and Treadling

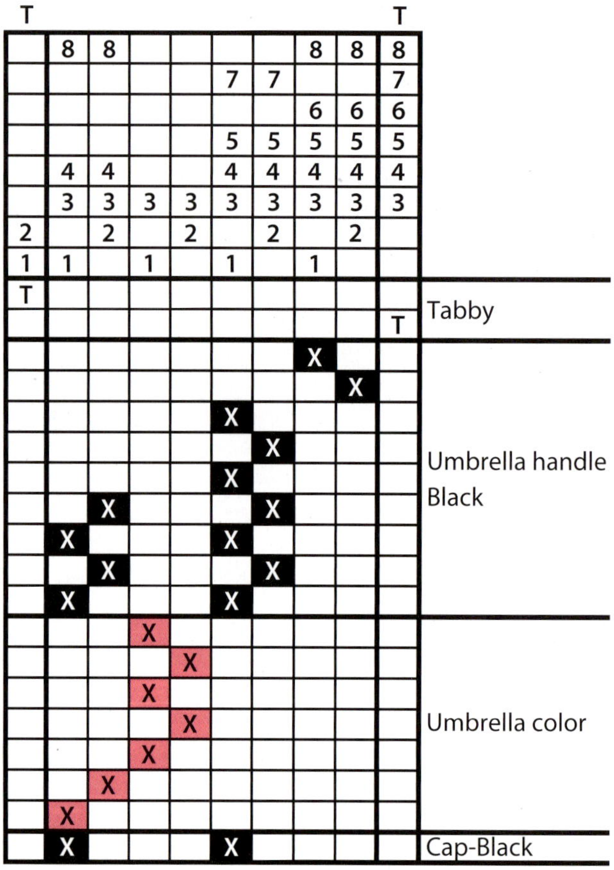

(Tie-up and treadling draft with numbered treadles 1–8, tabby T, and sections marked Tabby, Umbrella handle Black, Umbrella color, Cap-Black)

84 | UMBRELLAS FOR A RAINY DAY

Christmas Stockings

This set of towels will really make a statement at Christmas. Bake a loaf of your special bread and use one of these towels as gift wrapping! If your colors are different for the holidays, it would be easy to change the colors of the stockings. You could also use the rayon chenille for the white cuff and give a little more texture to your pieces.

Begin by weaving 3 inches (7.6 cm) of plain weave. I started the first towel with a row of Dark Red stockings and the second towel with a row of Winter Green stockings. After the White plain weave, you will weave your first row of stockings. Then weave 0.75 inches (1.9 cm) of plain weave followed by the next row, alternating colors. There are 9 rows of stockings in each towel. Weave another 3 inches (7.6 cm) of plain weave.

Now weave 4 passes of a high-contrast color, and then weave your second towel. Finish each towel with a rolled hem.

Note: Be sure to read Chapter 1, "The Most Important Chapter," before beginning any project in this book.

Dimensions: 17 × 24 inches (43.2 × 61 cm)

Warp
Sett: 20 epi, 10 dent reed, 2 threads per dent
Length: 3-yard (2.7-m) warp
Threads: 8/2 Cotton Clouds Aurora Earth
- White: 16 ends, 50 yards (45.7 m)
- Dark Red: 25 ends (includes 1 floating selvedge), 80 yards (73.2 m)
- Winter Green: 25 ends (includes 1 floating selvedge), 80 yards (73.2 m)
- Nile Green: 280 ends, 850 yards (777.2 m)

Weft
8/2 Cotton Clouds Aurora Earth
- Nile Green: 600 yards (548.6 m)
- White: 80 yards (73.2 m)
- Dark Red: 150 yards (137.2 m)
- Winter Green: 150 yards (137.2 m)

Threading
Alternate Motifs A and B: 7 times
Motif A: 1 time

		F							
			D						
				C					
					C				
						B			
A	A						A	A	A

Motif B
40 ends

3		3		3		3	
	2				2		
			1				1

Motif A
8 ends

Tie-up and Treadling

T									T	
	8	8	8	8					8	
	7	7							7	
									6	
							5	5	5	
					4	4	4	4	4	
	3	3	3	3	3	3	3	3	3	
2		2		2		2		2		
1	1		1		1		1			
T										Tabby
									T	
							X			Stocking color
								X		
					X					
						X				
						X				
			X							
				X						
			X							
	X									
		X								
	X									
		X								
	X									
		X								
	X									
		X								White Cuff
	X									
		X								
	X									

Treadling
Use tabby.

Spiders!!!

These are the only spiders I ever want to see in my house, whether in the kitchen or bathroom. They are just right for the Halloween season! The Orange warp stripe is based on twill threading, as all eight shafts had to be used for the spider pattern.

Begin by weaving 3 inches (7.6 cm) of plain weave in Orange cotton. Follow with 0.5 inches (1.3 cm) of White cotton. Then weave the first row of spiders. After you have finished this row, weave another 0.5 inches (1.3 cm) of plain weave in White. Next you will weave 0.5 inches (1.3 cm) of plain weave in Orange. Repeat until you have woven 5 rows of spiders. Finish your first towel by weaving another 3 inches (7.6 cm) of plain weave in Orange cotton. Weave 4 passes of a high-contrast color, and then weave your second towel.

Finish your towels with a rolled hem. Combine these with the Scary Skulls and the Jack-O'-Lanterns, and you will have a festive Halloween kitchen.

Note: Be sure to read Chapter 1, "The Most Important Chapter," before beginning any project in this book.

Dimensions: 17 × 24 inches (43.2 × 61 cm)

Warp
Sett: 20 epi, 10 dent reed, 2 threads per dent
Length: 3-yard (2.7-m) warp
Threads: 8/2 Cotton Clouds Aurora Earth
- White: 308 ends, 950 yards (868.7 m)
- Orange: 34 ends (includes 2 floating selvedges), 125 yards (114.3 m)

Weft
8/2 Cotton Clouds Aurora Earth
- White: 475 yards (434.3 m)
- Orange: 175 yards (160 m)
- Black: 325 yards (297.2 m)

Threading
Alternate Motifs A
and B: 7 times
Motif A: 1 time

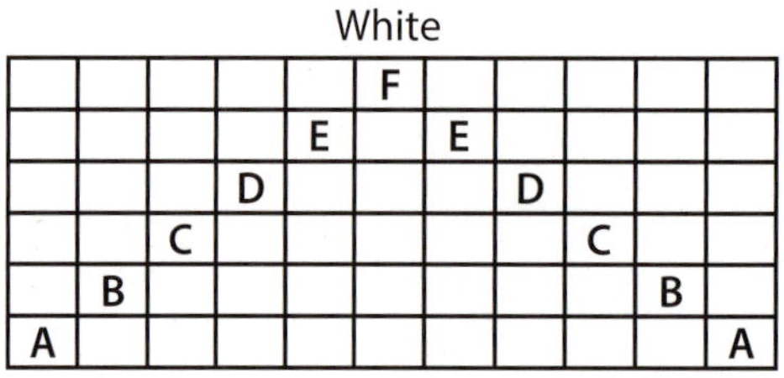

Motif B
44 ends

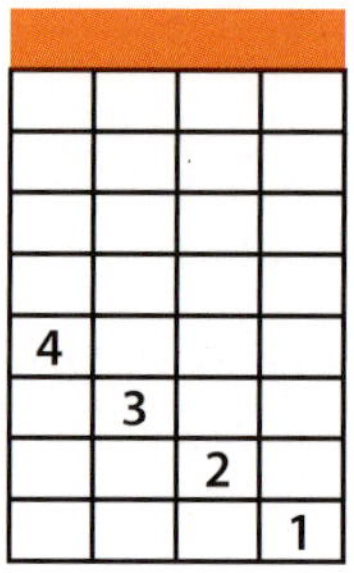

Motif A
4 ends

Tie-up and Treadling

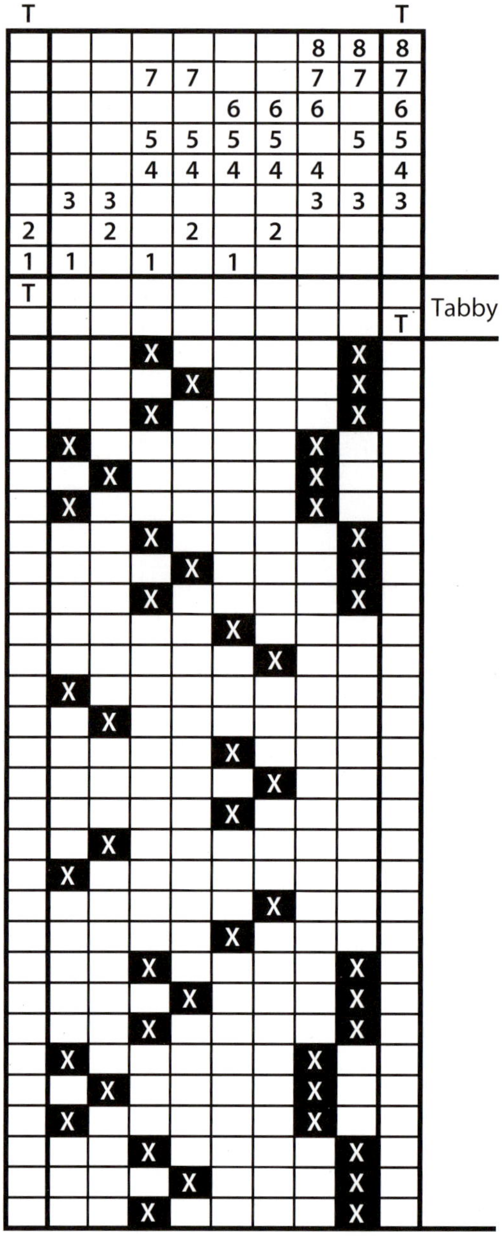

Treadling
Use tabby.

Tulips

This is the perfect set of towels for spring, as they are so bright and cheery! I wove one towel with just the red flowers but decided to use six different colors for the second towel. This pattern would also make a beautiful table runner or pillow.

Begin with 3 inches (7.6 cm) of plain weave in Kelly Green. Next weave 0.75 inches (1.9 cm) of White plain weave. Now you will weave the first row of tulips. After you have finished this row, weave another 0.75 inches (1.9 cm) of White plain weave. Repeat until you have woven 6 rows of tulips. Weave another 0.75 inches (1.9 cm) of White plain weave, and then follow with 3 inches (7.6 cm) of plain weave in Kelly Green. Weave 4 passes of a high-contrast color to separate the towels, and then weave your second towel.

Finish each towel with a rolled hem.

Note: Be sure to read Chapter 1, "The Most Important Chapter," before beginning any project in this book.

Dimensions: 16.5 × 25 inches (41.9 × 63.5 cm)

Warp
Sett: 20 epi, 10 dent reed, 2 threads per dent
Length: 3-yard (2.7-m) warp
Threads: 8/2 Cotton Clouds Aurora Earth
- Kelly Green: 26 ends (includes 2 floating selvedges), 90 yards (82.3 m)
- White: 312 ends, 950 yards (868.7 m)

Weft
8/2 Cotton Clouds Aurora Earth
- White: 450 yards (411.5 m)
- Kelly Green (borders): 350 yards (320 m)

Yardages are given per row of flower:
- Dark Red: 13 yards (11.9 m)
- Purple: 13 yards (11.9 m)
- Orange: 13 yards (11.9 m)
- Rose Red: 13 yards (11.9 m)
- Dark Turk: 13 yards (11.9 m)
- 8/2 Yarn Barn Cotton: Gold, 13 yards (11.9 m)

Motif
White

				E						
			D		D					
		C				C				
	B						B			
A	A	A						A	A	A

Motif 52 ends

Border

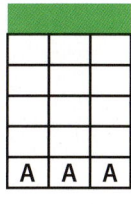

A	A	A

Border 12 ends

Threading
Border: 1 time
Motif: 6 times
Border: 1 time

Tie-up and Treadling

T								T	
								7	
	6	6			6	6		6	
				5	5	5	5	5	
	4	4	4			4	4	4	
	3	3	3	3	3	3	3	3	
2		2		2		2			
1	1		1		1		1		
T								T	Tabby
					X		X		Stem 3X
						X		X	
	X								Leaves
		X							
	X								
					X				
						X			
					X				
					X		X		Stem 2X
						X		X	
							X		Flower color
							X		
			X						
				X					
			X						
				X					
			X						
				X					
			X						
		X							
	X								
	X								

Treadling
Use tabby.

Blue Flowers

Spring has come with these lovely blue flowers. But I have also given you the yardage for individual rows of flowers if you want to have multiple colors. That would be a wonderful way to use up some of those small amounts of fiber. Do you have a wedding coming up? Weave a couple of sets of towels for the bride's kitchen in her colors! She will love it! You can also change the color of the flower center to whatever you like.

Begin your towel with 3 inches (7.6 cm) of plain weave in White cotton. Next you will weave 3 passes of Kelly Green, 2 passes of Empire Blue, and 3 passes of Kelly Green. Now weave 0.5 inches (1.3 cm) of White plain weave, and then weave your first row of flowers. Note that the tabby is indicated in the treadling. This is very important. When you get to the pink center, you will weave two different colors of pattern threads before you insert a tabby. Be sure to follow this approach, or your center won't look correct.

After you have woven your rows of flowers, weave another 0.5 inches (1.3 cm) of White plain weave, and then repeat the process starting with the horizontal stripes until you have woven 4 rows of flowers. End with the green/blue stripe and another 3 inches (7.6 cm) of White plain weave. Weave 4 passes of a high-contrast color to separate the towels, and then weave the second towel. Finish your towels with a rolled hem.

Note: Be sure to read Chapter 1, "The Most Important Chapter," before beginning any project in this book.

Dimensions: 16.5 × 23 inches (41.9 × 58.4 cm)

Warp
Sett: 20 epi, 10 dent reed, 2 threads per dent
Length: 3-yard (2.7-m) warp
Threads: 8/2 Cotton Clouds Aurora Earth
- White: 264 ends, 800 yards (731.5 m)
- Empire Blue: 18 ends, 75 yards (68.6 m)
- Kelly Green: 56 ends (includes 2 floating selvedges), 200 yards (182.9 m)

Weft
8/2 Cotton Clouds Aurora Earth
- White: 550 yards (502.9 m)
- Empire Blue: 225 yards (205.7 m)
- Kelly Green: 150 yards (137.2 m)
- Rose Red: 10 yards (9.1 m)

Or 22 yards (20.1 m) per row of flowers if you want multiple colors

Threading
Border: 1 time
Alternate Motifs A and B: 5 times
Motif A: 1 time
Border: 1 time

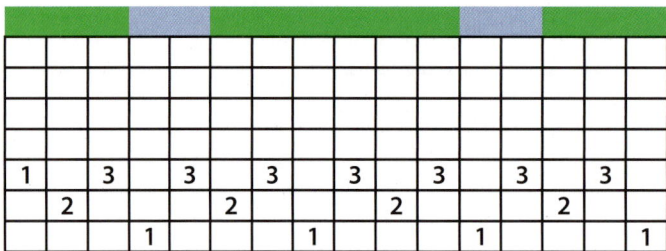

Border
16 ends

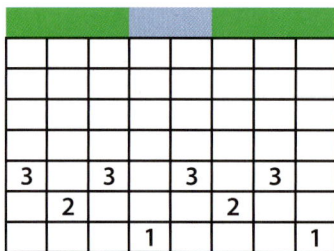

Motif A
44 ends

Motif B
8 ends

Tie-up and Treadling

T									T	
			7	7					7	
	6	6					6		6	
	5	5						5	5	
					4	4			4	
	3	3	3	3	3	3	3	3	3	
2		2		2		2				
1	1		1		1					
T										Tabby
									T	
	X				X					Pink
						X		X		Blue
T										Flower center
					X			X		
									T	
					X		X			
T										
						X	X			
									T	
					X		X			
T										
	X									
									T	Flower color
		X								
T										
	X									
									T	
	X				X					
T										
		X				X				
									T	
	X				X					
T										**End**

> **Treadling**
> Use tabby as indicated in chart.

T									T	
			7	7					7	
	6	6					6		6	
	5	5						5	5	
					4	4			4	
	3	3	3	3	3	3	3	3	3	
2		2		2		2				
1	1		1		1					
T										Tabby
									T	
	X				X					**Begin**
T										
		X				X				
									T	
	X				X					
T										
		X				X				
									T	
	X				X					
T										
						X				
									T	
					X					
T										
						X				Stem
									T	
	X									
T										
		X								
									T	
	X									
T										
	X				X					
									T	
		X				X				
T										
	X				X					
									T	
	X				X					
T										
		X				X				
									T	
	X				X					
T										
	X									
									T	
		X								
T										Flower color
	X									
									T	
					X		X			
T										
						X	X			
									T	
					X		X			
T										
					X			X		
									T	

Poppies

Poppies always remind me of my mother. She planted poppies one year and babied them along until they finally filled her flower bed. Such a beautiful flower, but I do wish they lasted longer. And now they will—in my kitchen! I used five different colors of red and pink, although you could use just one color.

Begin by weaving 3.5 inches (8.9 cm) of plain weave in Natural. Next you will begin to weave your first row of flowers, beginning with the stem of the flower. After you have finished the stem, weave the flower in your choice of colors. Note that the tabby is indicated in the center of the flower. If you begin with the correct tabby, you will automatically be using the one indicated at this point. You will put a flower color AND a pistil color before you place a tabby. Your flower color will enclose the pistil. This arrangement is reversed for the second half of the pistil, finishing with the tabby on the right.

Weave 1.75 inches (4.4 cm) of Natural plain weave and then your next row of flowers. Repeat until you have 5 rows of flowers for your towel. End with 3.5 inches (8.9 cm) of Natural plain weave. Weave 4 passes of a high-contrast color to separate your towels, and then weave the second towel. Finish your towels with a rolled hem.

Note: Be sure to read Chapter 1, "The Most Important Chapter," before beginning any project in this book.

Dimensions: 17 × 24 inches (43.2 × 61 cm)

Warp
Sett: 20 epi, 10 dent reed, 2 threads per dent
Length: 3-yard (2.7-m) warp
Threads: 8/2 Cotton Clouds Aurora Earth
- Natural: 308 ends, 950 yards (868.7 m)
- Winter Green: 34 ends (includes 2 floating selvedges), 120 yards (109.7 m)

Weft
8/2 Cotton Clouds Aurora Earth
- Natural: 600 yards (548.6 m)

Per row of flowers:
- Pistil: 8/2 Yarn Barn Cotton, Gold, 3 yards (2.7 m)
- Stem: 8/2 Cotton Clouds Aurora Earth, Winter Green, 20 yards (18.3 m)
- Flower: 8/2 Cotton Clouds Aurora Earth, 18 yards (16.5 m); colors used: Dark Red, Red, Rose Red, Beauty Rose, Lipstick

Threading
Alternate Motifs A
and B: 6 times
Motif A: 1 time

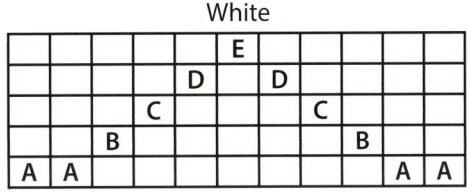

Motif B
44 ends

Motif A
12 ends

Tie-up and Treadling

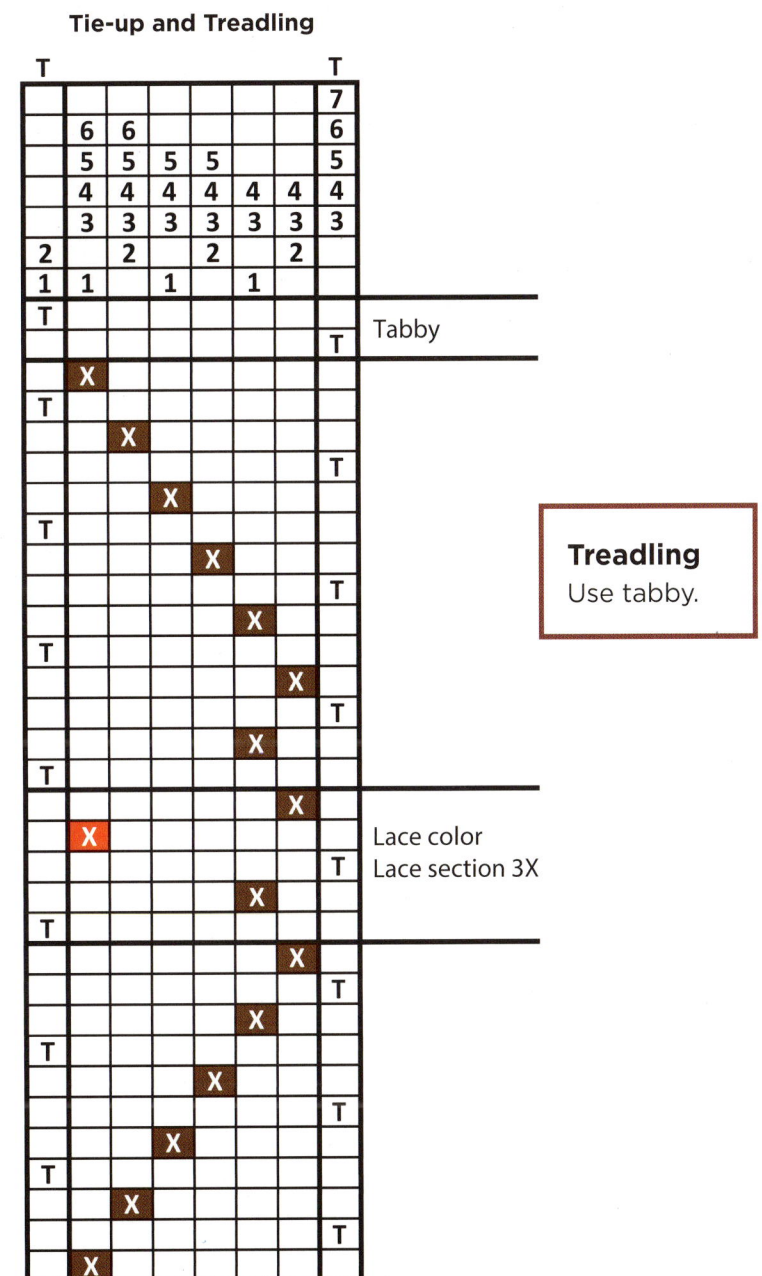

Tabby

Treadling
Use tabby.

Lace color
Lace section 3X

Snowflakes

Winter can be harsh! The cold, the snow, and being stuck inside! This set of towels will brighten the kitchen and make everything a bit more bearable. You can use any color for the background, but just be sure that your white snowflakes will shine. I used Dark Navy for the warp and Grape for the weft. Using the second color will soften the Dark Navy, and, when in a bright light, the two blended colors can be iridescent.

Begin with 3 inches (7.6 cm) of plain weave. Then you will weave your first row of snowflakes. After that, weave 0.5 inches (1.3 cm) of plain weave. Repeat this process until you have completed 9 rows of snowflakes. End your first towel with another 3 inches (7.6 cm) of plain weave. Weave 4 passes of plain weave in a high-contrast color to separate your towels, and then weave the second towel. Finish your towels with a rolled hem.

Note: Be sure to read Chapter 1, "The Most Important Chapter," before beginning any project in this book.

Dimensions: 17 × 24 inches (43.2 × 61 cm)

Warp
Sett: 20 epi, 10 dent reed, 2 threads per dent
Length: 3-yard (2.7-m) warp
Threads: 8/2 Cotton Clouds Aurora Earth
- Dark Navy: 332 ends, 1,000 yards (914.4 m)
- White: 10 ends (includes 2 floating selvedges), 35 yards (32 m)

Weft
8/2 Cotton Clouds Aurora Earth
- Grape: 580 yards (530.4 m)
- White: 400 yards (365.8 m)

Threading
Alternate Motifs A and B: 7 times
Motif A: 1 time

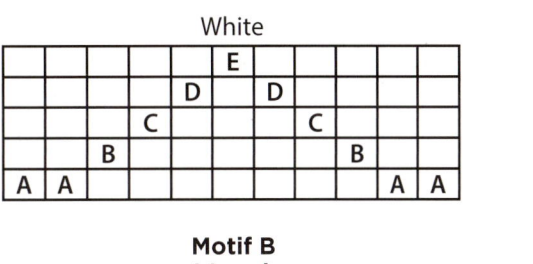

Motif B
44 ends

Motif A
4 ends

Tie-up and Treadling

Treadling
Use tabby.

CHRISTMAS TREES | 115

Birdhouses

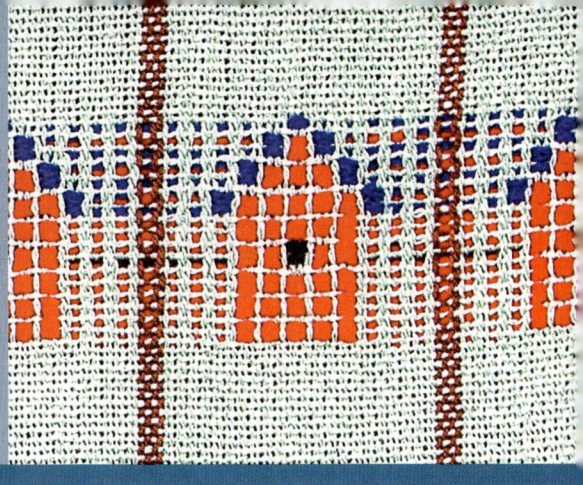

Birdhouses decorate our yards, and now they can decorate our kitchens as well! You could also change the pattern a bit to create a house instead of a birdhouse. Just extend the door! Now you have an option.

I chose to use Natural for the tabby to lighten the towel. But you can use Nile Green if you prefer. The yardage requirements were given as if you were weaving the same color birdhouses on your towels. But for the second towel I chose to use many different colors. This is a great way to use up small amounts of fiber. Again, you have an option.

Begin your towel with 3.75 inches (9.5 cm) of plain weave, and then you will begin to weave your first row of birdhouses. Do notice that there are areas where you will place two different pattern threads before you weave a tabby. Make sure that you follow these directions. After you have woven your first row of birdhouses, weave 1.5 inches (3.8 cm) of plain weave, and then begin your second row of birdhouses. Repeat until you have completed 7 rows of birdhouses. After the seventh row, weave 3.75 inches (9.5 cm) of plain weave.

Now weave 4 passes of a high-contrast color to separate your towels, and then weave the second towel. Finish your towels with a rolled hem.

Note: Be sure to read Chapter 1, "The Most Important Chapter," before beginning any project in this book.

Dimensions: 17 × 23 inches (43.2 × 58.4 cm)

Warp
Sett: 20 epi, 10 dent reed, 2 threads per dent
Length: 3-yard (2.7-m) warp
Threads: 8/2 Cotton Clouds Aurora Earth
- Nile Green: 308 ends, 950 yards (868.7 m)
- Dark Brown: 34 ends (includes 2 floating selvedges), 125 yards (114.3 m)

Weft
8/2 Cotton Clouds Aurora Earth
Tabby: Natural, 600 yards (548.6 m)
- Dark Red: 250 yards (228.6 m)
- Blue: 125 yards (114.3 m)
- Black: 30 yards (27.4 m)

Individual house color: allow 20 yards (18.3 m)

Threading
Alternate Motifs A and B: 7 times
Motif A: 1 time

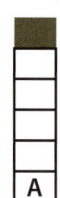

Motif A
4 ends

Motif B
44 ends

Treadling
Use tabby as indicated.

Tie-up and Treadling

			7	7	7			7	7	
		6		6	6				6	
		5	5		5	5			5	
		4	4	4		4	4	4	4	
		3	3	3	3	3	3	3	3	
	2									
	1	1	1	1	1	1	1	1		

Tabby section, Base of birdhouse, Hole, Top of birdhouse, Roof level 1, Roof level 2, Roof level 3, Roof peak

118 | BIRDHOUSES

Christmas Wreath

You can't hang this wreath on the door, but it is perfect for your kitchen. You could also make a table runner and matching placemats—or how about making some throw pillows to celebrate the season?

Begin your towel with 3.5 inches (8.9 cm) of White plain weave. Next weave 4 passes of Kelly Green, 4 passes of Dark Red, and 4 passes of Kelly Green. Follow this with 0.5 inches (1.3 cm) of White plain weave. Now weave your first row of wreaths followed with another 0.5 inches (1.3 cm) of White plain weave. Repeat this sequence until you have completed 5 rows of wreaths. End with the green/red/green sequence and another 3.5 inches (8.9 cm) of White plain weave.

Weave 4 passes of a high-contrast color, and then weave your second towel. Finish each towel with a rolled hem.

Note: Be sure to read Chapter 1, "The Most Important Chapter," before beginning any project in this book.

Dimensions: 16.5 × 26.5 inches (41.9 × 67.3 cm)

Warp
Sett: 20 epi, 10 dent reed, 2 threads per dent
Length: 3-yard (2.7-m) warp
Threads: 8/2 Cotton Clouds Aurora Earth
- White: 260 ends, 800 yards (731.5 m)
- Kelly Green: 50 ends (includes 2 floating selvedges), 175 yards (160 m)
- Dark Red: 24 ends, 85 yards (77.7 m)

Weft
8/2 Cotton Clouds Aurora Earth
- White: 600 yards (548.6 m)
- Dark Red: 145 yards (132.6 m)
- Kelly Green: 250 yards (228.6 m)

Threading
Alternate Motifs A and B: 5 times
Motif A: 1 time

White

Motif B
52 ends

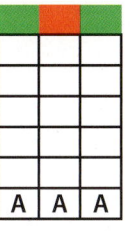

Motif A
12 ends

Tie-up and Treadling

Treadling
Use tabby.

Tabby

Tail of bow

Bow

Wreath

CHRISTMAS WREATH | 121

Candle and Holder

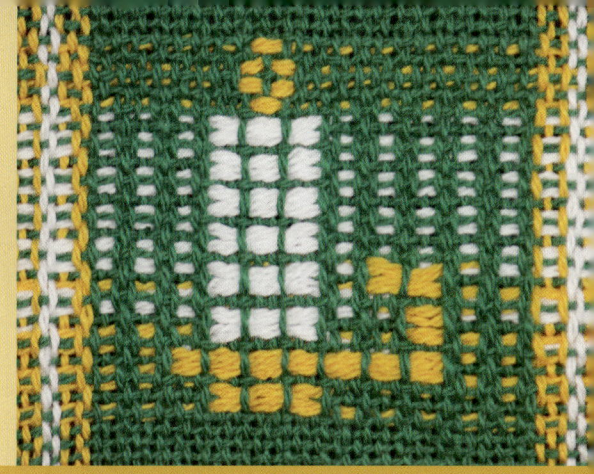

Candles are a staple in most homes. Since we have so many antiques, I decided to design a candle with a holder that would fit our décor. You could easily change the colors and make this a very festive towel for the Christmas holidays. You could also weave the candle without the holder and make your candles many different colors. This could be a towel that you use at a birthday party! So many ideas!

Begin your towel with 3.5 inches (8.9 cm) of Winter Green plain weave. Then weave 3 Gold, 2 White, and 3 Gold threads. Next weave 0.5 inches (1.3 cm) of plain weave in Winter Green. Now you will begin your first row of candles. I have indicated in the treadling where you will be placing two pattern threads with the tabby. If you begin with the correct tabby, you will automatically be using the one indicated at this point. Continue using a tabby throughout the image. After you have finished your row of candles, weave another 0.5 inches (1.3 cm) of Winter Green plain weave. Repeat the Gold–White–Gold color sequence and then continue until you have woven 6 rows of candles. Finally, weave another 3.5 inches (8.9 cm) of Winter Green plain weave. Weave 4 passes of a high-contrast color to separate the towels, and then weave your second towel just as the first towel. Finish your towels with a rolled hem.

Note: Be sure to read Chapter 1, "The Most Important Chapter," before beginning any project in this book.

Dimensions: 16.5 × 24.5 inches (41.9 × 62.2 cm)

Warp
Sett: 20 epi, 10 dent reed, 2 threads per dent
Length: 3-yard (2.7-m) warp
Threads:
8/2 Cotton Clouds Aurora Earth: White, 18 ends, 60 yards (54.9 m)
8/2 Cotton Clouds Aurora Earth: Winter Green, 264 ends, 800 yards (731.5 m)
8/2 Yarn Barn Cotton: Gold, 56 ends (includes 2 floating selvedges), 175 yards (160 m)

Weft
8/2 Cotton Clouds Aurora Earth: Winter Green, 600 yards (548.6 m)
8/2 Cotton Clouds Aurora Earth: White, 225 yards (205.7 m)
8/2 Yarn Barn Cotton: Gold, 250 yards (228.6 m)

Border
16 ends

Motif A
44 ends

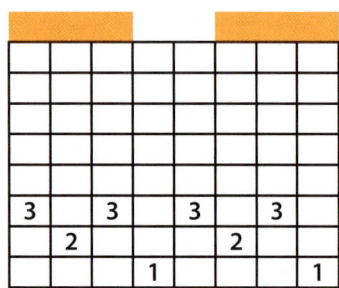

Motif B
8 ends

Threading
Border: 1 time
Alternate Motifs A and B: 5 times
Motif A: 1 time
Border: 1 time

Tie-up and Treadling

Tabby								
Base of holder								
Candle/handle								
Candle/handle								
Candle/handle								
Candle/handle								
Candle								
Flame								

Treadling
Use tabby.

124 | CANDLE AND HOLDER

Shamrocks

Here is a lucky shamrock for my Irish friends to hang in their kitchen or bathroom. For those who really celebrate their Irish heritage, how about using the green, white, and orange colors of the Irish flag as your warp? Just make sure the green you use for the shamrock is darker than the one you use in the stripe so your shamrock still stands proud.

Begin your towel with 4 inches (10.2 cm) of White plain weave. Then weave 4 passes of Kelly Green followed by 0.5 inches (1.3 cm) of White plain weave. Next you will weave your first row of shamrocks. Follow with another 0.5 inches (1.3 cm) of White plain weave. Repeat until you have woven 5 rows of shamrocks. Weave another 4 passes of Kelly Green plain weave, followed by 4 inches (10.2 cm) of White plain weave. Weave 4 passes of a high-contrast color, and then weave your second towel. Finish your towels with a rolled hem.

Note: Be sure to read Chapter 1, "The Most Important Chapter," before beginning any project in this book.

Dimensions: 17.5 × 24.5 inches (44.5 × 62.2 cm)

Warp	Weft
Sett: 20 epi, 10 dent reed, 2 threads per dent **Length:** 3-yard (2.7-m) warp **Threads:** 8/2 Cotton Clouds Aurora Earth • White: 300 ends, 925 yards (845.8 m) • Kelly Green: 50 ends (includes 2 floating selvedges), 175 yards (160 m)	8/2 Cotton Clouds Aurora Earth • White: 550 yards (502.9 m) • Kelly Green: 400 yards (365.8 m)

Threading
Alternate Motifs A and B: 5 times
Motif A: 1 time

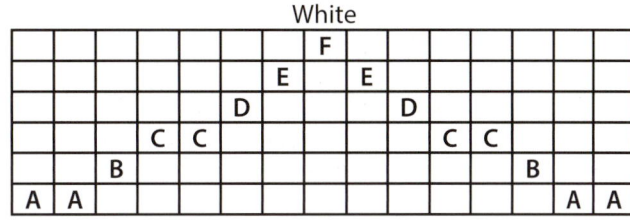

Motif B
60 ends

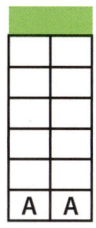

Motif A
8 ends

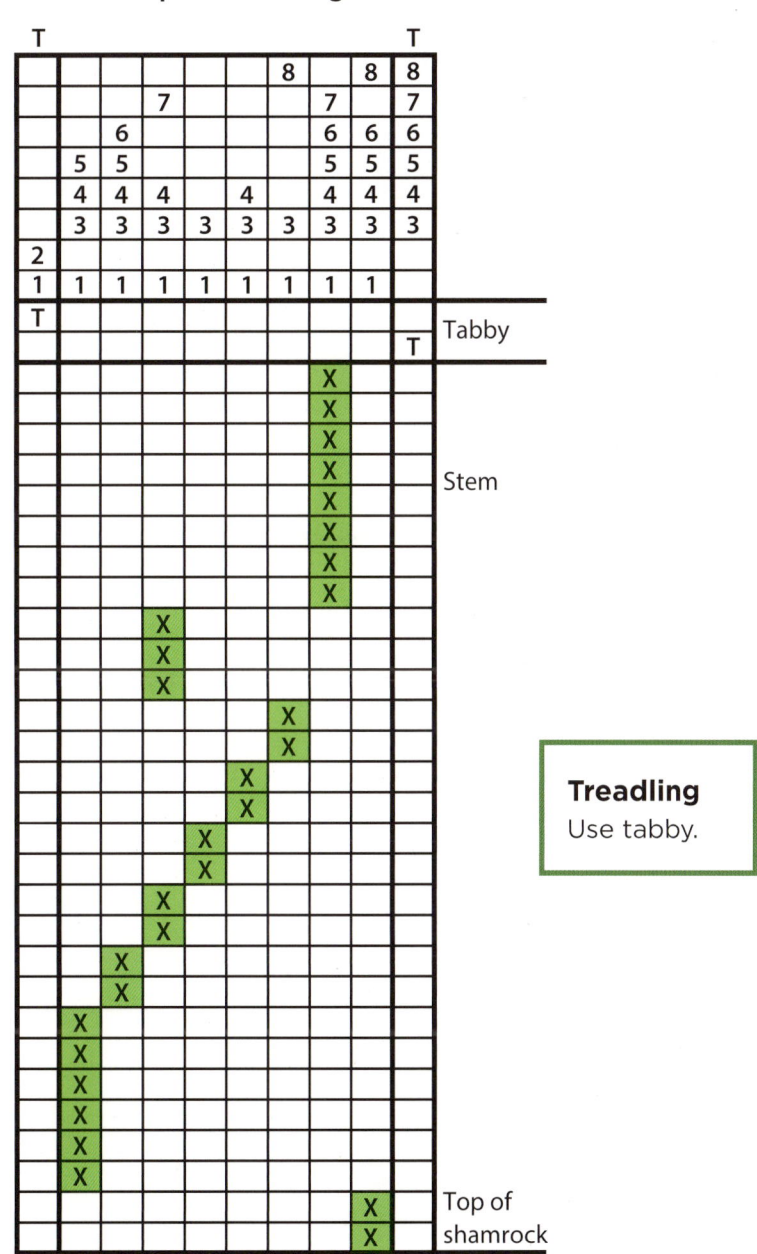

Treadling
Use tabby.

Scottish Thistle

The Scottish thistle has been the national emblem for Scotland since the 1200s. It is strong and hardy, just like the Scottish people. This plant displays a stunning purple flower, is very resilient, and covers the Scottish countryside. Legend has it that an invading soldier stepped on the prickly thorns and cried out, alerting the Scottish soldiers that they were about to be attacked.

This is an easy pattern to weave. I even managed to work in a simple plaid. If you have a Scottish background or want to make a set for a Scottish friend, it would be easy to change the colors and number of threads that are used in the plaid.

Begin by weaving 3 inches (7.6 cm) of Natural plain weave. The plaid horizontal stripes are woven in plain weave as follows:

6 Dark Red–3 Copen Blue–6 Kelly Green–3 Copen Blue–6 Dark Red

After you have woven the stripe, weave 0.5 inches (1.3 cm) of Natural plain weave. Then you will weave the first row of thistles. Follow with another 0.5 inches (1.3 cm) of Natural plain weave and follow with a set of horizontal stripes. Repeat until you have woven 4 rows of thistles. Finish with another set of horizontal stripes and 3 inches (7.6 cm) of Natural plain weave. Weave 4 passes of a high-contrast thread to separate your towels, and then weave your second towel. Finish your towels with a rolled hem.

Note: Be sure to read Chapter 1, "The Most Important Chapter," before beginning any project in this book.

Dimensions: 16.5 × 25 inches (41.9 × 63.5 cm)

Warp
Sett: 20 epi, 10 dent reed, 2 threads per dent
Length: 3-yard (2.7-m) warp
Threads: 8/2 Cotton Clouds Aurora Earth
- Natural: 176 ends, 550 yards (502.9 m)
- Dark Red: 82 ends (includes 2 floating selvedges), 250 yards (228.6 m)
- Copen Blue: 40 ends, 140 yards (128 m)
- Kelly Green: 40 ends, 140 yards (128 m)

Weft
8/2 Cotton Clouds Aurora Earth
- Natural: 460 yards (420.6 m)
- Kelly Green: 230 yards (210.3 m)
- Dark Red: 60 yards (54.9 m)
- Copen Blue: 30 yards (27.4 m)
- Purple: 60 yards (54.9 m)

Threading
Alternate Motifs A and B: 4 times
Motif A: 1 time

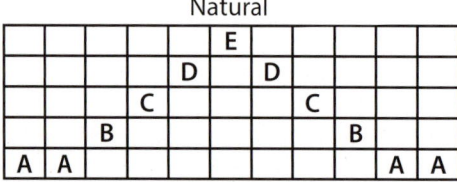

Motif B
44 ends

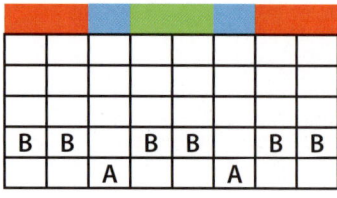

Motif A
32 ends

Tie-up and Treadling

Treadling
Use tabby.

Tabby

Base of thistle

Thistle flower

130 | SCOTTISH THISTLE

Owls

My daughter-in-law collects articles that have owls on them, so this set of towels is just for her! While I stuck with more natural colors for this set, you could really brighten them up using primary colors. They would make an adorable baby blanket!

Begin with 3.5 inches (8.9 cm) of Nile Green plain weave and then 4 passes of Dark Green plain weave. Follow with 0.5 inches (1.3 cm) of Nile Green plain weave, and then you will weave your first row of owls. Note the places where you will be placing two complete pattern threads, followed by a tabby. In the area of the eye, you will be placing three complete sets of pattern threads. After you have completed your first row of owls, follow with another 0.5 inches (1.3 cm) of Nile Green plain weave. Repeat this process until you have woven 6 rows of owls.

Weave another 4 passes of Dark Green plain weave, followed by another 3.5 inches (8.9 cm) of Nile Green plain weave. Then weave 4 passes of a high-contrast color to separate your towels, and then weave the second towel. Finish your towels with a rolled hem.

Note: Be sure to read Chapter 1, "The Most Important Chapter," before beginning any project in this book.

Dimensions: 17 × 24 inches (43.2 × 61 cm)

Warp
Sett: 20 epi, 10 dent reed, 2 threads per dent
Length: 3-yard (2.7-m) warp
Threads: 8/2 Cotton Clouds Aurora Earth
- Nile Green: 308 ends, 950 yards (868.7 m)
- Dark Green: 34 ends (includes 2 floating selvedges), 110 yards (100.6 m)

Weft
8/2 Cotton Clouds Aurora Earth
- Natural: 60 yards (54.9 m)
- Cinnamon: 100 yards (91.4 m)
- Black: 15 yards (13.7 m)
- Light Brown: 250 yards (228.6 m)
- Nile Green: 600 yards (548.6 m)
- Dark Green: 30 yards (27.4 m)

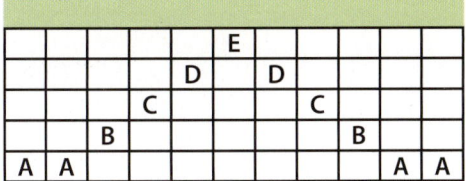

Motif B
44 ends

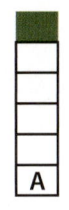

Motif A
4 ends

Threading
Alternate Motifs A and B: 7 times
Motif A: 1 time

Tie-up and Treadling

Treadling
Use tabby.

OWLS | 133

Sheep

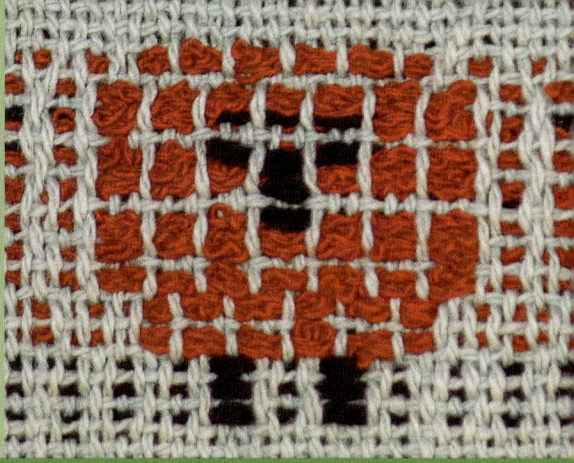

These towels are a complete flock of sheep in all colors—just like in nature! We know spinners and weavers are always looking at the different colors of wool to get just the right one for their project. You could weave your towels with all of the colors I used or use just one color. Your choice! I used cotton bouclé so that my sheep had a bit of texture. Feel free to use regular 8/2 cotton if you wish. The bouclé is 8/2, so use a double strand for the pattern thread.

Begin with 3.5 inches (8.9 cm) of Nile Green tabby. Then weave your first row of sheep. Be sure to carefully read the treadling pattern. You will weave 1.5 inches (3.8 cm) of Nile Green tabby between each row of sheep. There are 8 rows of sheep per towel. After you have woven your last row of sheep, weave another 3.5 inches (8.9 cm) of plain weave. Then weave 4 passes of a high-contrast color to separate your towels, and weave your second towel. Finish your towels with a rolled hem.

Now . . . the colors I used for the sheep. The 8/2 cotton bouclé colors were White, Black, Rust, and Beige. The 8/2 cotton colors for the face and legs were Black, White, and Rust. While I used the same colors for the face and legs within the individual sheep, you could weave black legs and brown faces. Make these sheep your own. Yardage needed is given *per sheep*, so you will need to decide how you want your towels to look so you know how much yardage is needed.

Note: Be sure to read Chapter 1, "The Most Important Chapter," before beginning any project in this book.

Dimensions: 17 × 24.5 inches (43.2 × 62.2 cm)

Warp
Sett: 20 epi, 10 dent reed, 2 threads per dent
Length: 3-yard (2.7-m) warp
Threads: 8/2 Cotton Clouds Aurora Earth
- Nile Green: 308 ends, 950 yards (868.7 m)
- Natural: 34 ends (includes 2 floating selvedges), 125 yards (114.3 m)

Weft
Tabby: 8/2 Cotton Clouds Aurora Earth: Nile Green, 600 yards (548.6 m)
UKI Supreme Cotton Bouclé: Black, White, Beige, Rust
- *Per sheep:* 10 yards (9.1 m)
8/2 Cotton Clouds Aurora Earth
- *Eyes/mouth/legs, per sheep:* 10 yards (9.1 m)

Threading
Alternate Motifs A and B: 7 times
Motif A: 1 time

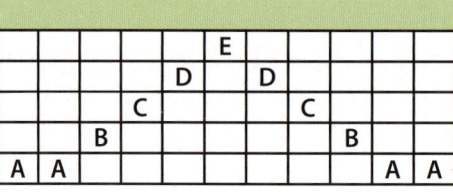

Motif B
44 ends

Motif A
4 ends

Tie-up and Treadling

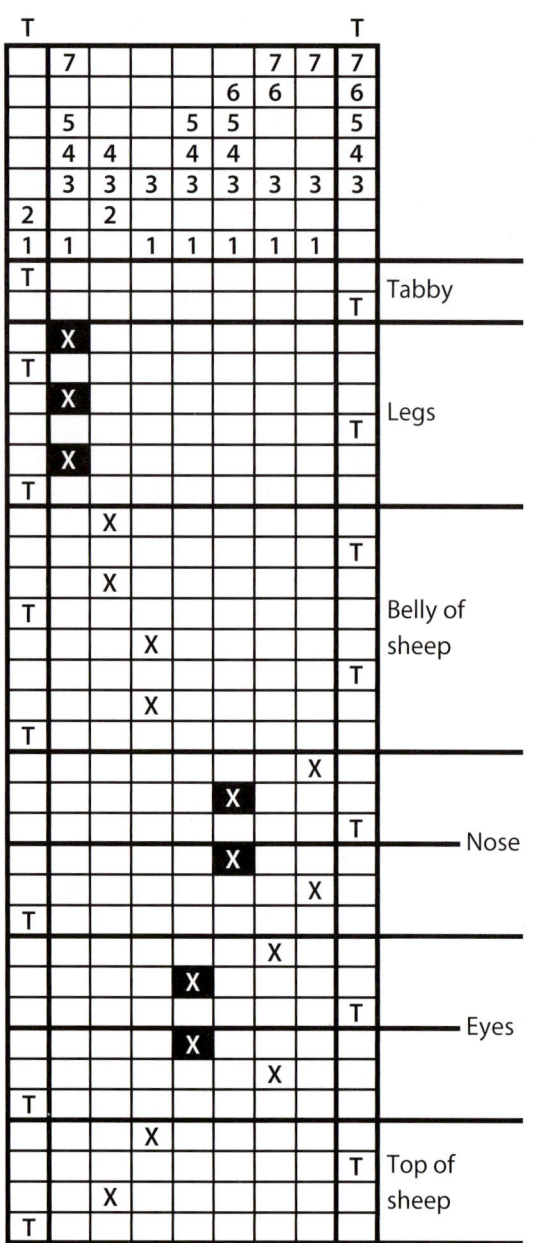

Treadling
Use tabby.

Butterflies

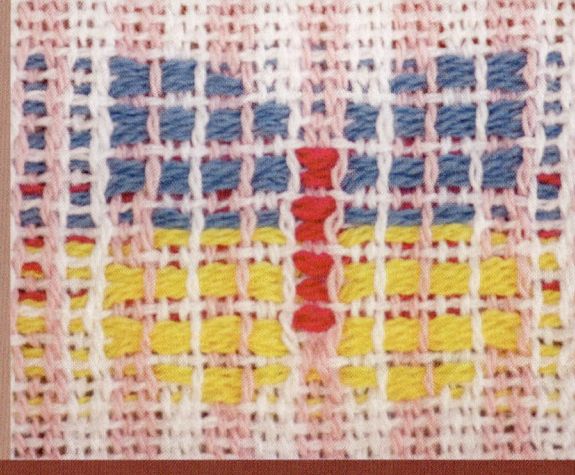

Spring has arrived with this influx of butterflies. I shared a picture of this project with a friend, and she's ready to weave a special blanket for her granddaughter.

Don't let the stripes overwhelm you. You can always just use a plain warp. I began each towel alternating 4 Special Pink and 4 White tabbies for 3.5 inches (8.9 cm), ending with 4 White. Then I began the first row of butterflies. Just use White for the tabby in the motif. It is much easier, and the color change isn't visible. After you have finished the first row, your tabby shuttle will be on the right-hand side of the project, so you will need to do 5 passes of White, which will get your shuttle on the correct side. Now alternate 4 Special Pink, 4 White, 4 Special Pink, and 4 White, and you are ready to begin another butterfly. There are 8 rows of butterflies per towel.

Notice in the treadling that there are places where you will be putting 2 complete pattern threads before you weave a tabby thread. Be sure that you follow the treadling draft carefully.

After you have woven the last motif, again you will need to weave 5 White passes. Then alternate 4 Special Pink and 4 White until you have 3.5 inches (8.9 cm). Weave a high-contrast color to separate your towels, and then weave the second towel. Finish your towels with a rolled hem.

I used multiple colors for the butterflies. This is a great set of towels to use up small amounts of leftover material. The yardages given are per wing, so if you want your butterflies to all be the same, you will need to do some math.

Note: Be sure to read Chapter 1, "The Most Important Chapter," before beginning any project in this book.

Dimensions: 17.4 × 24.5 inches (44.2 × 62.2 cm)

Warp
Sett: 20 epi, 10 dent reed, 2 threads per dent
Length: 3-yard (2.7-m) warp
Threads: 8/2 Cotton Clouds Aurora Earth
- White: 172 ends, 525 yards (480 m)
- Special Pink: 178 ends (includes 2 floating selvedges), 550 yards (502.9 m)

Weft
8/2 Cotton Clouds Aurora Earth
Tabby:
- Special Pink: 125 yards (114.3 m)
- White: 475 yards (434.3 m)

Per butterfly:
- *Per wing:* 10 yards (9.1 m)
- *Per butterfly body:* 10 yards (9.1 m)

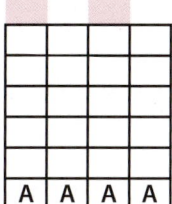
Border 2
16 ends

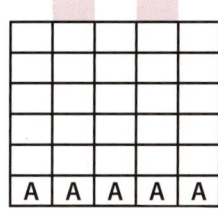
Motif B
20 ends

Motif A
36 ends

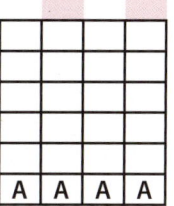
Border 1
16 ends

Threading
Border 1: 1 time
Alternate Motifs A
 and B: 5 times
Motif A: 1 time
Border 2: 1 time

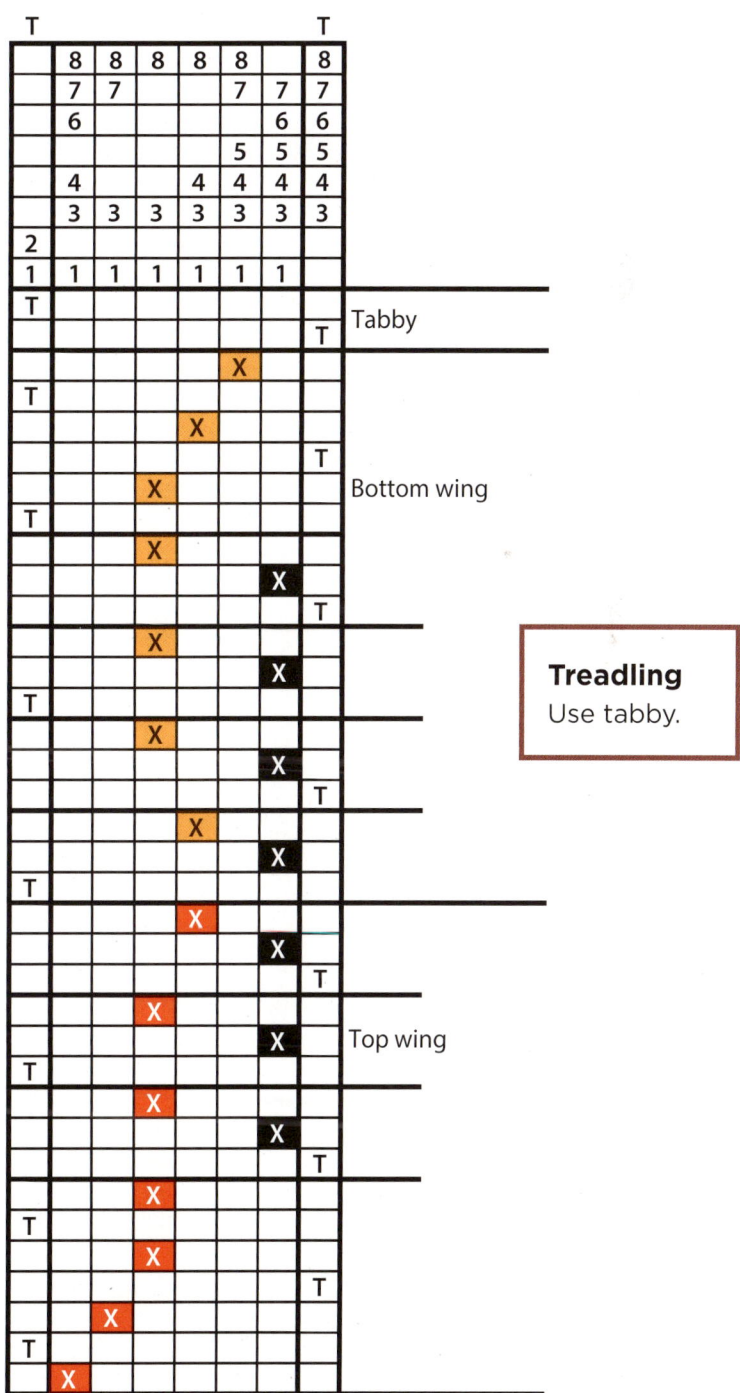

Tie-up and Treadling

Treadling
Use tabby.

Snowmen

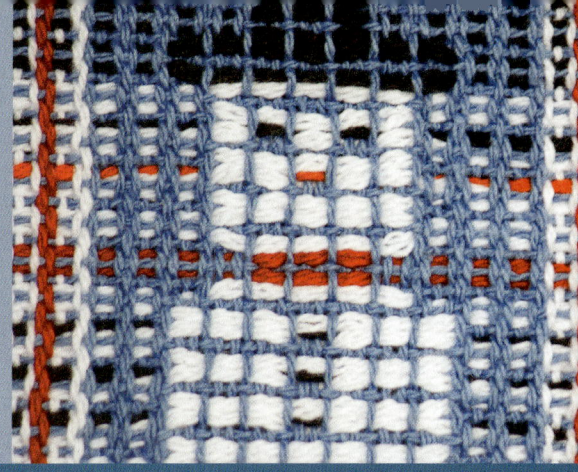

This is the best way to build a snowman! No freezing fingers and toes, no snow tracked into the house, and—best of all—these snowmen don't melt! It's an ideal set of towels for the winter months or as a gift for that person who collects snowman memorabilia.

Begin your towel with 4 inches (10.2 cm) of Empire Blue tabby followed by 3 White–2 Dark Red–3 White tabby stripes. Next weave 0.5 inches (1.3 cm) of Empire Blue tabby, and then you will begin to weave your first row of snowmen. Note that there are areas where you will be placing two pattern threads before weaving the tabby. After you have woven your first row of snowmen, weave another 0.5 inches (1.3 cm) of Empire Blue tabby. Repeat the process until you have woven 5 rows of snowmen. Weave 3 White–2 Dark Red–3 White stripes and a final 4 inches (10.2 cm) of Empire Blue tabby. Next weave 4 passes of a high-contrast color to separate your towels, and then weave your second towel. Finish each towel with a rolled hem.

Note: Be sure to read Chapter 1, "The Most Important Chapter," before beginning any project in this book.

Dimensions: 16.4 × 24.5 inches (41.7 × 62.2 cm)

Warp
Sett: 20 epi, 10 dent reed, 2 threads per dent
Length: 3-yard (2.7-m) warp
Threads: 8/2 Cotton Clouds Aurora Earth
- White: 48 ends (includes 2 floating selvedges), 175 yards (160 m)
- Dark Red: 18 ends, 75 yards (68.6 m)
- Empire Blue: 264 ends, 825 yards (754.4 m)

Weft
8/2 Cotton Clouds Aurora Earth
- Empire Blue: 550 yards (502.9 m)
- Dark Red: 50 yards (45.7 m)
- Orange: 15 yards (13.7 m)
- White: 250 yards (228.6 m)
- Black: 125 yards (114.3 m)

Threading
Border 1: 1 time
Alternate Motifs A and B: 5 times
Motif A: 1 time
Border: 1 time

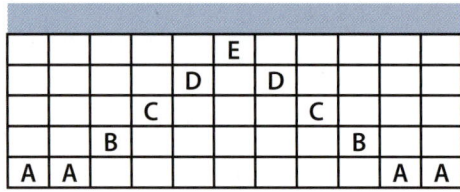

Motif A
44 ends

Border
12 ends

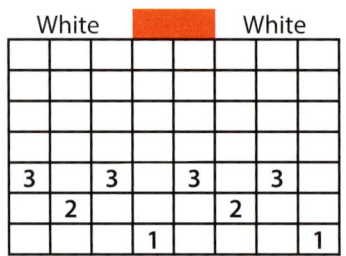

Motif B
8 ends

Treadling
Use tabby.

Tie-up and Treadling

142 | SNOWMEN

Cupcakes

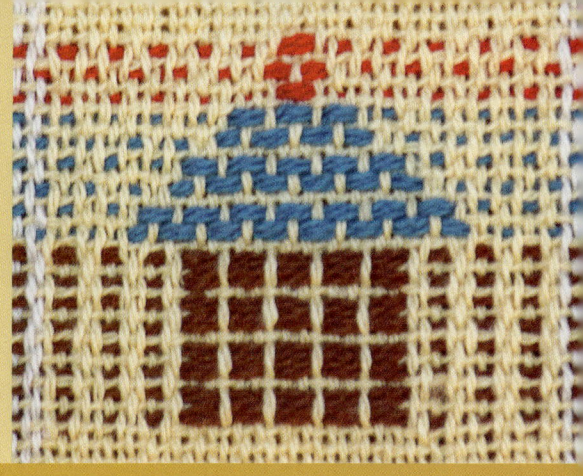

These are the perfect cupcakes—there are no calories! How great is that? I used 4 different colors for the icing, but you can use more than that or just one color. Individually, allow 7 yards (6.4 m) for each row of cupcakes.

Begin your first towel with 3.5 inches (8.9 cm) of plain weave in Champagne. Then weave 0.5 inches (1.3 cm) of plain weave in Natural. Weave your first row of cupcakes using Natural as your tabby, and follow with 0.5 inches (1.3 cm) of plain weave in Natural. Now change your tabby to Champagne and follow the same pattern to weave your second row of cupcakes. After you have woven 8 rows of cupcakes, you will finish with 3.5 inches (8.9 cm) of plain weave in Natural. Icing colors are alternated in the towels. Weave 4 passes of a high-contrast thread, and then weave your second towel. Finish each towel with a rolled hem.

You have a bonus pattern that creates a lit candle (page 123)! This would be great for a birthday party either as a towel or as a table runner. A special birthday for a 4-year-old? Weave a towel with 4 cupcakes and candles. A special birthday that would require many candles? Weave towels or a runner with the needed number of cupcakes and candles. No need to set the house on fire! All of my cupcakes are chocolate, which is my favorite. Make these your own!

Note: Be sure to read Chapter 1, "The Most Important Chapter," before beginning any project in this book.

Dimensions: 16 × 24 inches (40.6 × 61 cm)

Warp
Sett: 20 epi, 10 dent reed, 2 threads per dent
Length: 3-yard (2.7-m) warp
Threads: 8/2 Cotton Clouds Aurora Earth
- Champagne: 150 ends (includes 2 floating selvedges), 475 yards (434.3 m)
- Natural: 176 ends, 550 yards (502.9 m)

Weft
8/2 Cotton Clouds Aurora Earth
- Champagne: 300 yards (274.3 m)
- Natural: 300 yards (274.3 m)
- Light Brown: 160 yards (146.3 m)
- Dark Red: 50 yards (45.7 m)
- Special Purple: 30 yards (27.4 m)
- Beauty Rose: 30 yards (27.4 m)
- Light Orange: 30 yards (27.4 m)
- Dark Turk: 30 yards (27.4 m)

Threading
Border 1: 1 time
Alternate Motifs A and B: 3 times
Motif A: 1 time
Border: 1 time

Motif B
44 ends

Motif A
44 ends
Natural

Border
8 ends

Tie-up and Treadling

Tabby
Cupcake
Icing
Candle
Flame

Treadling
Use tabby.

Tabby
Cupcake
Icing
Cherry

CUPCAKES | 145

Dapper Dachshund

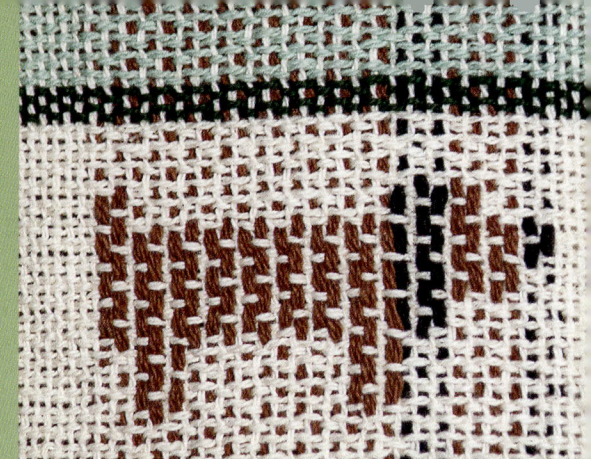

These dogs may be dachshunds, but you could shorten the body and create a sweet little dog. Of course, you can also make the body longer just for fun. The listed colors can easily be changed. Did one of your children or grandchildren draw their dog using a rainbow of colors? How about re-creating that image in a towel! It would be such a fun gift.

Begin your towel with 3.5 inches (8.9 cm) of plain weave. I used only the Natural color for the tabby for both towels. Feel free to change this approach. Next you will weave your first row of dogs. After you have finished, weave 1.5 inches (3.8 cm) of Natural plain weave. For your second row of dogs, use the second combination of colors. Repeat until you have woven 6 rows of dogs, weaving 3.5 inches (8.9 cm) of plain weave after the sixth and last row. Weave 4 passes of a high-contrast color to separate your towels, and then weave your second towel. Finish your towels with a rolled hem.

Note: Be sure to read Chapter 1, "The Most Important Chapter," before beginning any project in this book.

Dimensions: 16.5 × 27 inches (41.9 × 68.6 cm)

Warp
Sett: 20 epi, 10 dent reed, 2 threads per dent
Length: 3-yard (2.7-m) warp
Threads: 8/2 Cotton Clouds Aurora Earth
- Natural: 160 ends, 500 yards (457.2 m)
- Nile Green: 120 ends, 400 yards (365.8 m)
- Dark Green: 50 ends (includes 2 floating selvedges), 175 yards (160 m)

Weft
8/2 Cotton Clouds Aurora Earth
Dog 1:
- Light Brown: 180 yards (164.6 m)
- Black: 30 yards (27.4 m)

Dog 2:
- Rust: 180 yards (164.6 m)
- Chocolate: 30 yards (27.4 m)

Tabby: Natural, 575 yards (525.8 m)

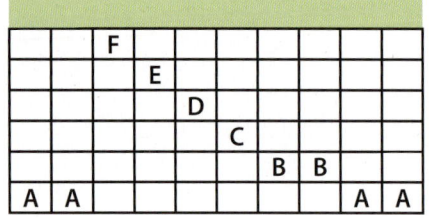

Motif C
40 ends

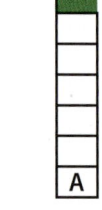

Motif B
4 ends

Natural

Motif A
40 ends

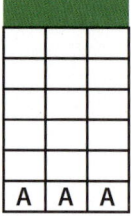

Border
12 ends

Threading
Border: 1 time
Motifs A, B, C, B: 3 times
Motif A: 1 time
Border: 1 time

Tie-up and Treadling

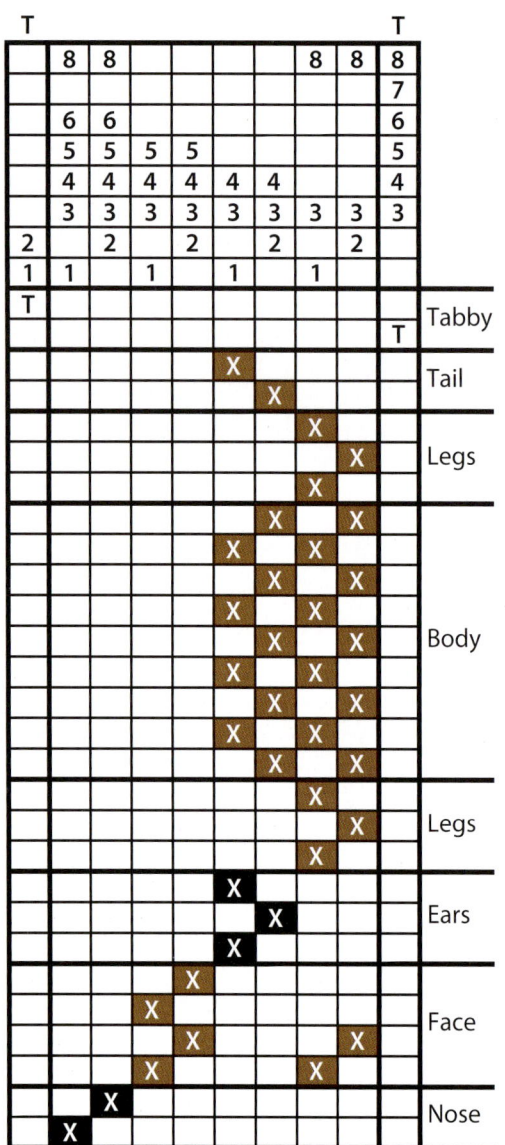

Treadling
Use tabby.

Cows

Having been raised on a dairy farm, I just couldn't resist the temptation to create a cow. In one towel the cows are brown and white to represent Guernsey cows—my favorite. But the second towel is black and white for Holsteins. You could change the colors to create Jerseys, Brown Swiss, or even beef cattle.

Begin your towels with 3.5 inches (8.9 cm) of plain weave in Natural. Then you will weave your first row of cows. Note that you will be using a tabby throughout the towels, but there are sections where two pattern threads are placed before a tabby is thrown. In these sections, you will notice that the tabby is indicated. If you have started with the correct tabby, you will automatically be using the correct tabby in these sections. After the first row of cows, weave 1.5 inches (3.8 cm) of Natural plain weave. Repeat until you have woven 7 rows of cows. Finish with 3.5 inches (8.9 cm) of Natural plain weave. Now weave 4 passes of a high-contrast color to separate your towels, and then weave your second towel. Finish your towels with a rolled hem.

Note: Be sure to read Chapter 1, "The Most Important Chapter," before beginning any project in this book.

Dimensions: 17 × 24 inches (43.2 × 61 cm)

Warp

Sett: 20 epi, 10 dent reed, 2 threads per dent
Length: 3-yard (2.7-m) warp
Threads: 8/2 Cotton Clouds Aurora Earth
- Natural: 312 ends, 950 yards (868.7 m)
- Dark Green: 30 ends (includes 2 floating selvedges), 100 yards (91.4 m)

Weft

8/2 Cotton Clouds Aurora Earth
- Dark Brown: 100 yards (91.4 m)
- Black: 100 yards (91.4 m)
- Peach: 100 yards (91.4 m)
- White: 50 yards (45.7 m)
- Beauty Rose: 20 yards (18.3 m)

Threading
Alternate Motifs A
and B: 6 times
Motif A: 1 time

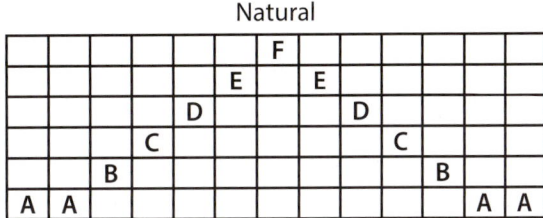

Motif B
52 ends

Motif A
4 ends

Tie-up and Treadling

Treadling
Use tabby.

COWS | 151

Honeybees

These little bees are cute, and they won't sting you, although they won't provide any honey for you either. This would be a wonderful set of towels for a friend who is a beekeeper. Begin your towel with 3.5 inches (8.9 cm) of plain weave. Next you will weave your first row of bees. I chose to carry my thread along the side, but it does require juggling 4 shuttles. Note that in the treadling chart there are sections where the appropriate tabby is indicated. If you have started with the correct tabby, your tabby will automatically be in the right position. After the row of bees, weave 1.5 inches (3.8 cm) of plain weave and then repeat until you have woven 9 rows of bees. After the last row of bees, weave 3.5 inches (8.9 cm) of plain weave. Now weave 4 passes of a high-contrast color to separate the towels, and then weave the second towel. Finish your towels with a rolled hem.

Note: Be sure to read Chapter 1, "The Most Important Chapter," before beginning any project in this book.

Dimensions: 17 × 26.5 inches (43.2 × 67.3 cm)

Warp
Sett: 20 epi, 10 dent reed, 2 threads per dent
Length: 3-yard (2.7-m) warp
Threads: 8/2 Cotton Clouds Aurora Earth
- Natural: 58 ends (includes 2 floating selvedges), 200 yards (182.9 m)
- Winter Green: 288 ends, 875 yards (800.1 m)

Weft
8/2 Cotton Clouds Aurora Earth
- Black: 175 yards (160 m)
- Natural: 120 yards (109.7 m)
- Maize: 95 yards (86.9 m)
- Winter Green: 600 yards (548.6 m)

Threading
Alternate Motifs A and B: 6 times
Motif A: 1 time

					E	E							
				D			D						
			C					C					
		B							B				
A	A									A	A		A	A

Motif B
48 ends

Natural

Motif A
8 ends

Tie-up and Treadling

Treadling
Use tabby.

	T			T	
		7	7	7	7
	6	6			6
	5			5	5
	4			4	4
	3	3	3	3	3
2					
1	1	1	1	1	

T						Tabby
				T	
X						Beg. of bee
X					
X					
X					
X						Beg. of wing
	X				
T					
X					
		X			
				T	
X						Center of wing
		X			
T					
X					
		X			
				T	
X						End of wing
	X				
T					
	X					Top of head
			X			Antennae
			X		

154 | HONEYBEES

Vegetable Garden

My type of gardening—no weeds! Seriously, this is a fun towel for any kitchen, especially in the summer when all of that fresh produce is being canned and frozen. Begin your towels with 4 inches (10.2 cm) of plain weave. Next you will begin to weave your rows of vegetables. It doesn't really matter what sequence you choose. My sequence was carrots, turnips, tomatoes, corn, onions, and then beets. Be sure to use a tabby throughout. Instead of a variety of vegetables, you could weave just one type.

Between each row of vegetables, weave 1.5 inches (3.8 cm) of plain weave. End your towel with another 4 inches (10.2 cm) of plain weave and then 4 passes of a high-contrast thread to separate the towels. Now you can weave your second towel.

A note about the corn: You will see that there are five areas where there are two pattern threads before you place the tabby. If you have started with the correct tabby, you will automatically be using the indicated tabby.

Note: Be sure to read Chapter 1, "The Most Important Chapter," before beginning any project in this book.

Dimensions: 16.5 × 23 inches (41.9 × 58.4 cm)

Warp
Sett: 20 epi, 10 dent reed, 2 threads per dent
Length: 3-yard (2.7-m) warp
Threads: 8/2 Cotton Clouds Aurora Earth
- Winter Green: 46 ends (includes 2 floating selvedges), 150 yards (137.2 m)
- Nile Green: 288 ends, 900 yards (823 m)

Weft
8/2 Cotton Clouds Aurora Earth
Tabby: Nile Green, 550 yards (502.9 m)
- Tomato: Dark Red, 20 yards (18.3 m)
- Base of turnip: Polo Tan, 15 yards (13.7 m)
- Top of turnip: Magenta, 15 yards (13.7 m)
- Corn: Maize, 35 yards (32 m)
- Onion: Cinnamon, 25 yards (22.9 m)
- Carrot: Orange, 30 yards (27.4 m)
- Beet: Lipstick, 30 yards (27.4 m)
- Leaves: Winter Green, 100 yards (91.4 m)

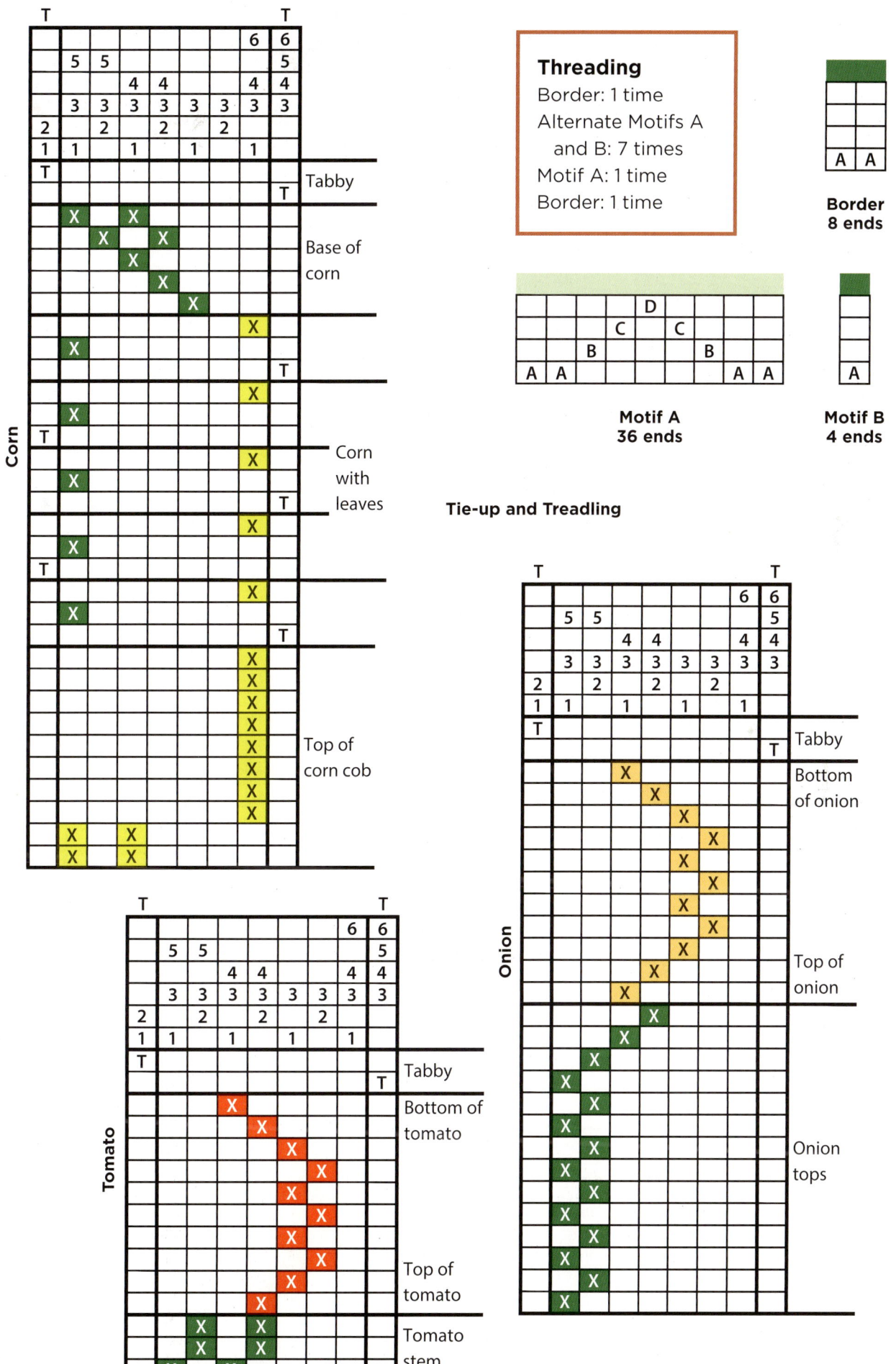

VEGETABLE GARDEN | 157

Treadling
Use tabby throughout; read text for details.

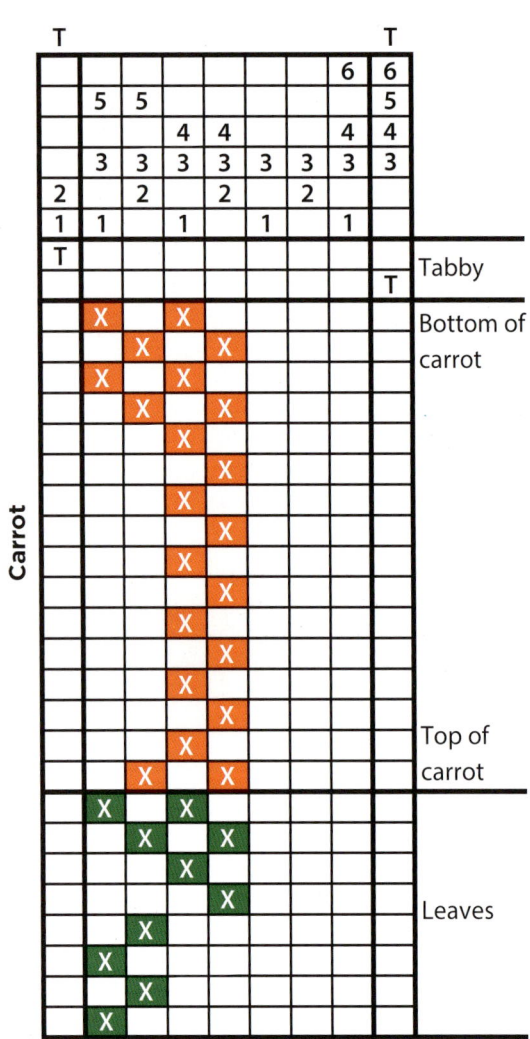
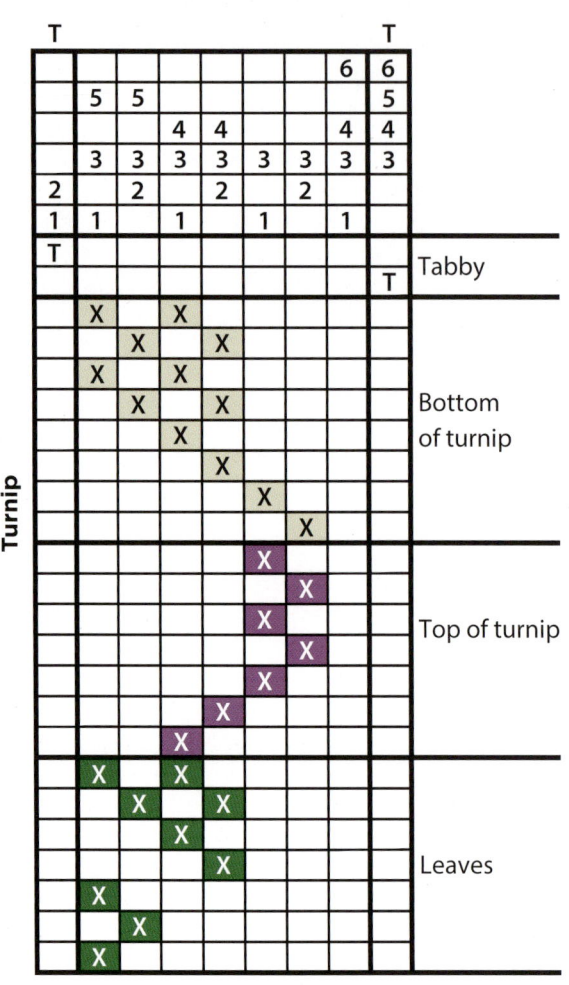
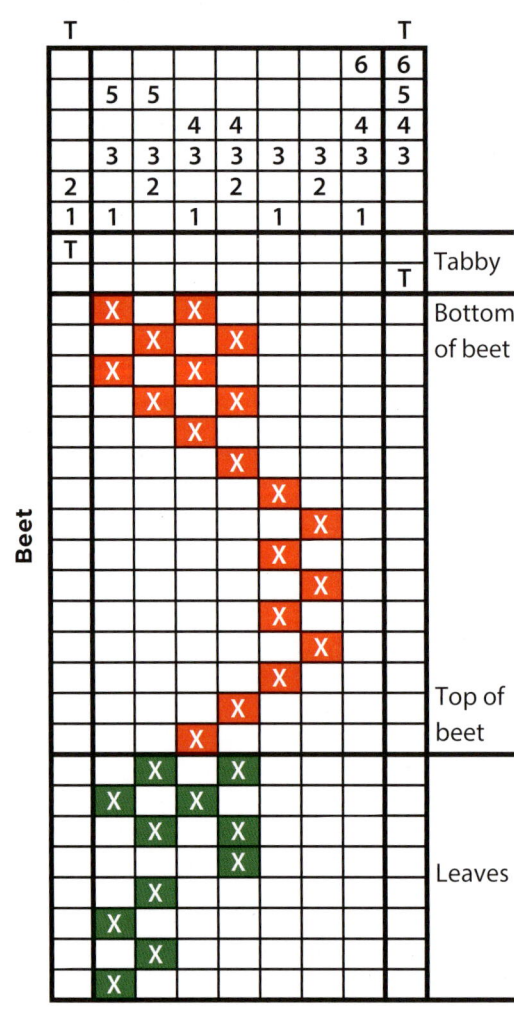

Tie-up and Treadling

158 | VEGETABLE GARDEN

Happy Hour

This is the ideal towel for a bartender or a beer connoisseur! You could easily change the color of the beer to match your favorite IPA(s). Begin your towel with 3.5 inches (8.9 cm) of plain weave in Turk. Then you will weave your first row of beer mugs. There are sections where two pattern threads are placed before the tabby is used. In these sections, the correct tabby is indicated. If you begin with the correct tabby, you will automatically be using the indicated tabby at this point. I used White cotton bouclé for the head on the beer. This thread gives the head some texture. You can use White 8/2 cotton, but I really like the effect of the bouclé. After you have woven your first row of towels, weave another 2 inches (5.1 cm) of plain weave. Repeat until you have 5 rows of beer mugs. Follow with 3.5 inches (8.9 cm) of plain weave. Weave 4 passes of a high-contrast thread, and then weave your second towel. Finish the towels with rolled hems.

Note: Be sure to read Chapter 1, "The Most Important Chapter," before beginning any project in this book.

Dimensions: 16.5 × 24.5 inches (41.9 × 62.2 cm)

Warp
Sett: 20 epi, 10 dent reed, 2 threads per dent
Length: 3-yard (2.7-m) warp
Threads: 8/2 Cotton Clouds Aurora Earth
- Turk: 280 ends, 875 yards (800.1 m)
- White: 58 ends (includes 2 floating selvedges), 200 yards (182.9 m)

Weft
8/2 Cotton Clouds Aurora Earth: White, 200 yards (182.9 m)

8/2 Yarn Barn Cotton: Gold, 180 yards (164.6 m)

Yarn Barn Bouclé: White, 60 yards (54.9 m)

8/2 Cotton Clouds Aurora Earth: Turk, 550 yards (502.9 m)

Threading
Border: 1 time
Alternate Motifs A and B: 4 times
Motif A: 1 time
Border: 1 time

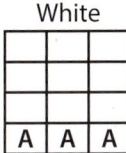

Border
12 ends

Motif A
56 ends

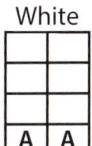

Motif B
8 ends

Treadling
Use tabby.

Tie-up and Treadling

Teddy Bears

How fun are these towels? They would be great burping cloths for that new grandchild. Adapt the design for a matching baby blanket! Begin your towel with 3.5 inches (8.9 cm) of plain weave in Baby Blue. Next weave 4 passes of Blue followed with 0.5 inches (1.3 cm) of plain weave in Baby Blue. Now you are ready to weave your first row of teddy bears. Use a tabby throughout the motif. You will notice that there are sections in the treadling where you will place two pattern threads and then a tabby. Also notice that the specific tabby is indicated in these sections. If you begin the teddy bears with the correct tabby, you will automatically be using the indicated tabby. After you have woven the teddy bears, weave another 0.5 inches (1.3 cm) of plain weave. Repeat this process until you have complete 6 rows of teddy bears. Follow with 4 passes of Blue and then another 3.5 inches (8.9 cm) of plain weave in Baby Blue. Weave 4 passes of a high-contrast color to separate your towels, and weave the second towel. Finish your towels with a rolled hem.

Note: Be sure to read Chapter 1, "The Most Important Chapter," before beginning any project in this book.

Dimensions: 17 × 25.5 inches (43.2 × 64.8 cm)

Warp
Sett: 20 epi, 10 dent reed, 2 threads per dent
Length: 3-yard (2.7-m) warp
Threads: 8/2 Cotton Clouds Aurora Earth
- Baby Blue: 308 ends, 950 yards (868.7 m)
- Blue: 34 ends (includes 2 floating selvedges), 125 yards (114.3 m)

Weft
8/2 Cotton Clouds Aurora Earth
- Baby Blue: 600 yards (548.6 m)
- Rust: 250 yards (228.6 m)
- Black: 60 yards (54.9 m)

Threading
Alternate Motifs A
and B: 7 times
Motif A: 1 time

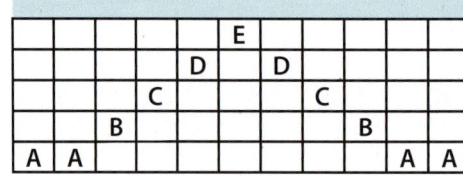

Motif B
44 ends

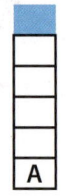

Motif A
4 ends

Tie-up and Treadling

Treadling
Use tabby.

164 | TEDDY BEARS

Mushrooms

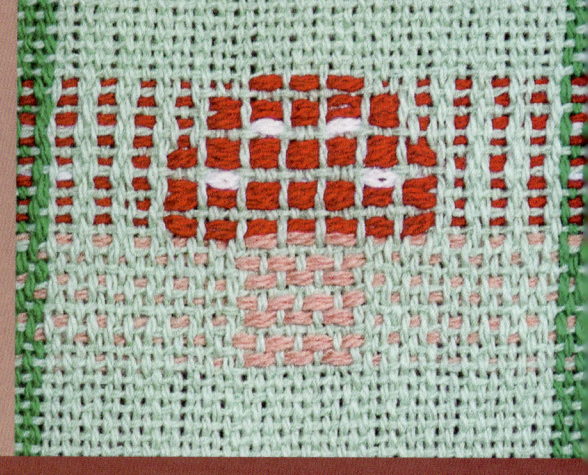

Many years ago, I had a friend who decorated her kitchen with all sorts of mushroom-themed items. It was so bright and colorful. Mushroom pieces are still enjoyed by many, so this set of towels is for them. You could easily change the colors of the mushroom caps and make your towels even more colorful.

Begin your towel with 3.5 inches (8.9 cm) of plain weave in Mint Green. Then weave 4 passes of Winter Green followed by 0.5 inches (1.3 cm) of Mint Green, all in plain weave. Now you are ready to weave your first row of mushrooms. Use a tabby throughout the motif. There are two sections where two pattern threads are placed before you weave your tabby. The correct tabby is indicated, and if you begin your mushrooms with the appropriate one, you will automatically be using the indicated tabby. After you finish your row of mushrooms, weave 0.5 inches (1.3 cm) of plain weave in Mint Green. Then repeat until you have woven 7 rows of mushrooms. Finish with another 4 passes of Winter Green and then 3.5 inches (8.9 cm) of Mint Green plain weave. Weave 4 passes of a high-contrast color to separate your towels, and then weave your second towel. Finish your towels with a rolled hem.

Note: Be sure to read Chapter 1, "The Most Important Chapter," before beginning any project in this book.

Dimensions: 17 × 24 inches (43.2 × 61 cm)

Warp
Sett: 20 epi, 10 dent reed, 2 threads per dent
Length: 3-yard (2.7-m) warp
Threads:
8/2 Yarn Barn Cotton: Mint Green, 312 ends, 950 yards (868.7 m)
8/2 Cotton Clouds Aurora Earth: Winter Green, 30 ends (includes 2 floating selvedges), 100 yards (91.4 m)

Weft
8/2 Yarn Barn Cotton: Mint Green, 600 yards (548.6 m)
8/2 Cotton Clouds Aurora Earth
- White: 30 yards (27.4 m)
- Peach: 100 yards (91.4 m)
- Dark Red: 120 yards (109.7 m)
- Winter Green: 35 yards (32 m)

Threading
Alternate Motifs A and B: 6 times
Motif A: 1 time

Motif B
52 ends

Motif A
4 ends

Mint Green

Treadling
Use tabby.

Tie-up and Treadling

Tabby	
Stem	
Base of mushroom	
First set of dots	
Center of mushroom	
Second set of dots	
Top of mushroom	

Pigs

Pigs come in all shapes and sizes, and now people have pet pigs. This set of towels is for the pig lovers! These pigs are pink, but you could weave them in different colors for fun or to match your child's favorite stuffed pig toy.

Begin the towel with 3.5 inches (8.9 cm) of plain weave. Then weave your first row of pigs. The tabby is indicated in areas where two or three pattern threads are placed before a tabby is thrown. If you begin with the correct tabby, you will automatically be using the one indicated at this point. After you have woven your first row of pigs, weave 1.5 inches (3.8 cm) of plain weave. Repeat until you have 7 rows of pigs, and then weave 3.5 inches (8.9 cm) of plain weave. Weave 4 passes of a high-contrast thread to separate the towels, and then weave your second towel. Finish your towels with a rolled hem.

Note: Be sure to read Chapter 1, "The Most Important Chapter," before beginning any project in this book.

Dimensions: 17 × 24 inches (43.2 × 61 cm)

Warp
Sett: 20 epi, 10 dent reed, 2 threads per dent
Length: 3-yard (2.7-m) warp
Threads: 8/2 Cotton Clouds Aurora Earth
- Polo Tan: 312 ends, 950 yards (868.7 m)
- Special Pink: 30 ends (includes 2 floating selvedges), 100 yards (91.4 m)

Weft
8/2 Cotton Clouds Aurora Earth
- Black: 50 yards (45.7 m)
- Beauty Rose: 250 yards (228.6 m)
- Special Pink: 65 yards (59.4 m)
- Polo Tan: 600 yards (548.6 m)

Threading
Alternate Motifs A and B: 6 times
Motif A: 1 time

Motif B
52 ends

Motif A
4 ends

Tie-up and Treadling

Treadling
Use tabby.

Tabby	
Bottom of head	
Beg. of nose	
Second pass of nose	
Nose with Black nostrils	
Top of nose	
Bridge	
Eyes	
Eyes	
Forehead	
Ears	

Red or White?

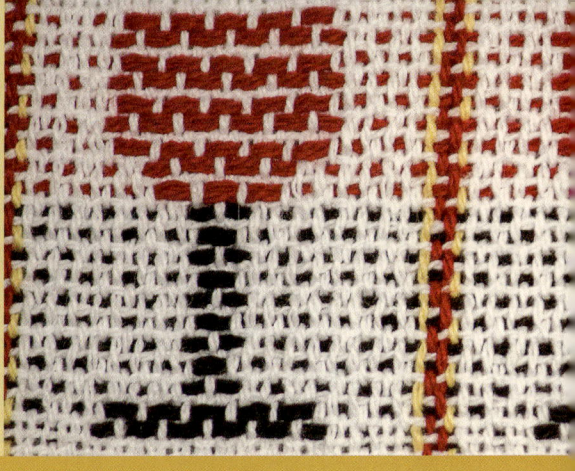

We have a towel for the beer drinkers—and now we have a towel for the wine drinkers! I chose two colors for the wine, but you can easily change those or include more colors. These motifs are very easy to weave since there are no insets. Begin with 3.5 inches (8.9 cm) of plain weave, and then weave your first row of wine glasses. After your motif row, weave 1.5 inches (3.8 cm) of plain weave. Repeat until you have woven 7 rows of wine glasses. End with another 3.5 inches (8.9 cm) of plain weave. Weave 4 passes of a high-contrast thread, and then weave your second towel. Finish your towels with a rolled hem.

I began with the red wine and alternated the colors, ending with another row of red wine. You could make your towels all one color or only put one row of glasses at each end.

Note: Be sure to read Chapter 1, "The Most Important Chapter," before beginning any project in this book.

Dimensions: 16.5 × 26 inches (41.9 × 66 cm)

Warp
Sett: 20 epi, 10 dent reed, 2 threads per dent
Length: 3-yard (2.7-m) warp
Threads: 8/2 Cotton Clouds Aurora Earth
- Champagne: 28 ends (includes 2 floating selvedges), 100 yards (91.4 m)
- Lipstick: 18 ends, 60 yards (54.9 m)
- White: 288 ends, 875 yards (800.1 m)

Weft
8/2 Cotton Clouds Aurora Earth
- Black: 175 yards (160 m)
- Champagne: 60 yards (54.9 m)
- Lipstick: 80 yards (73.2 m)
- White: 550 yards (502.9 m)

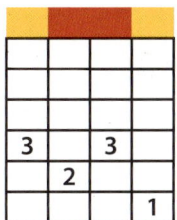

Motif B
4 ends

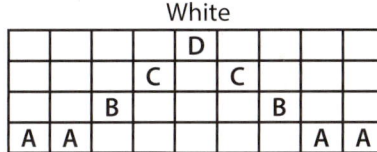

Motif A
36 ends

Border
8 ends

Threading
Border: 1 time
Alternate Motifs A
 and B: 7 times
Motif A: 1 time
Border: 1 time

Tie-up and Treadling

Treadling
Use tabby.

Tabby
Bottom of glass
Stem
Top of glass

RED OR WHITE? | 173

Alpacas and Llamas

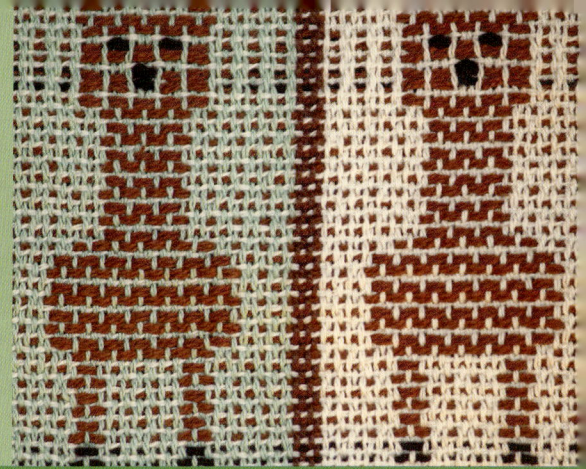

Alpacas and llamas are such delightful animals. And the fiber they create is a spinner's and weaver's delight! So now we have a set of towels that will allow us to have one of our favorite animals in our home. I used natural colors for my animals, but you could be creative and use a rainbow of colors, or maybe just give them all blue eyes! Begin your towel with 3 inches (7.6 cm) of plain weave in Nile Green. Then weave 0.5 inches (1.3 cm) of plain weave in Natural. Now you will weave your first row of alpacas/llamas. Be sure to use a tabby, and yes, you will be depressing two treadles for one of the tabbies. After you have woven your animals, weave another 0.5 inches (1.3 cm) of plain weave in Natural. Now change to the Nile Green thread and repeat. Continue until you have woven 5 rows of animals.

I used five different colors for the alpacas/llamas, making a dark-colored nose, mouth, and eyes for the light-colored animals and light-colored eyes, nose, and mouth for the dark-colored animals. You have plenty of yardage to decide what colors to use. Notice in the treadling section with the eyes, mouth, and nose that the tabby is indicated. If you begin with the correct tabby, you will automatically be using the indicated tabby at this point. You will be weaving two pattern threads before placing the tabby. After you have woven your fifth row of animals, weave 0.5 inches (1.3 cm) of plain weave in Natural and another 3 inches (7.6 cm) of tabby in Nile Green. Weave 4 rows of a high-contrast color to separate your towels, and then weave your second towel. Finish your towels with a rolled hem.

Note: Be sure to read Chapter 1, "The Most Important Chapter," before beginning any project in this book.

Dimensions: 17 × 25 inches (43.2 × 63.5 cm)

Warp
Sett: 20 epi, 10 dent reed, 2 threads per dent
Length: 3-yard (2.7-m) warp
Threads: 8/2 Cotton Clouds Aurora Earth
- Nile Green: 176 ends, 550 yards (502.9 m)
- Light Brown: 34 ends (includes 2 floating selvedges), 120 yards (109.7 m)
- Natural: 132 ends, 425 yards (388.6 m)

Weft
8/2 Cotton Clouds Aurora Earth
- Nile Green: 600 yards (548.6 m)
- Natural: 600 yards (548.6 m)
- Chocolate: 85 yards (77.7 m)
- Light Brown: 85 yards (77.7 m)
- Cinnamon: 85 yards (77.7 m)
- Light Cocoa: 85 yards (77.7 m)
- Black: 100 yards (91.4 m)

Natural

Motif C
44 ends

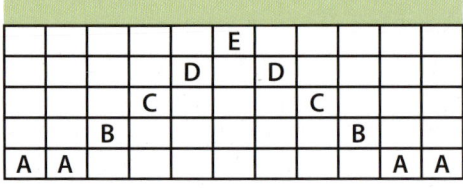

Motif B
44 ends

Motif A
4 ends

Threading
Alternate Motifs A, B, A, C: 3 times
Motifs A, B, A: 1 time

Tie-up and Treadling

Treadling
Use tabby.

Region	Repeats
Tabby	
Hooves	
Legs	3X
Beg. of Body	
Body	3X
End of body	
Neck	5X
Beg. of head	
Mouth	
Nose	
Bridge	
Eyes	
Top of head	
Ears	